MELANIE ASHFIELD

80s Kid

A memoir of growing up in the last decade before technology took over

Contents

Welcome to a World of Modernity and
Kitchen Gadgets   1

Berni Inn   13

'Can He Eat Crisps?'   23

Feminism in the 1980s; Still an Awfully
Long Way to Go   29

'Proper Winters'   36

School Days   44

Birthday Parties   52

Practical Jokes   56

Family Holidays Before They Were 'Foreign'   64

More 'Foreigners'   68

Midnight Feast   74

Miss McCoughney Gets a Boyfriend   82

Weddings and Celebrations   88

Secondary School is an Anti-Climax   96

Linda Lusardi Lives With Benny Hill   106

Teenage Dating   111

Clubbing With Fake ID   117

Fad Diets and Expanding People   121

The 'Foreign Holiday'   126

What Teenagers Did Before Technology and
Social Media   136

Champagne Charlies and The 'Offy'   145

Parties and Bad Hair   150

Everyone Wants to be a Supermodel   157

The Pursuit of Pleasure   163

I've Seen the Future and It Works   170

Welcome to a World of Modernity and Kitchen Gadgets

I was four years old when we landed at the yellow brick semi in 1980. I can see us now, rocking up in Dad's red Volkswagen Beetle, with my twin brother Tony and me dancing around minus seatbelts, in the warm recess on top of the engine, bizarrely located in the boot (as our grandad, a Second World War-veteran, liked to remind us: all Germans were imbeciles.) I think we were belting out Pink Floyd's 'Another Brick in the Wall' in squeaky voices, with debatable lyrics (there is still a cassette somewhere with Tony and me shrieking about 'another prick in the wall' and 'dark sandcastles in the classroom').

The significance of our move to the Birmingham suburbs for our parents, baby boomers who had grown up on a postwar slum clearance council estate and an inner-city Edwardian semi respectively, was they had really made it. Alan and Teresa Jones, born and bred working-class Brummies, like their parents and grandparents before them, were entering a new decade where they could start to live the dream of bettering their lot. They were part of the postwar 'baby boomer' generation, the first generation that was not constricted to remain in the social class they were born into. They could be educated out of it, marry out of it, be lucky enough to win on the Littlewoods Pools or Premium Bonds or, as in my dad's case, you could simply graft your way out of it. First homes were usually family-sized, rather than the matchbox-sized starter homes of today, and could be snapped up by working-class couples, usually on the man's salary alone, ready to be filled with children, for whom the wife had already planned to give up work permanently in preparation for.

Our new yellow house was on the outskirts of Birmingham, near the chocolate-box village of Bournville, a town planner's dream of cottage-style dwellings with sash windows, neatly-manicured front gardens and privet hedges. These were mostly rented by the Cadbury factory workers. Greenery and landscaping were in so much abundance, you could be forgiven for thinking you were in the countryside, rather than the outskirts of a grey industrial town. However, because Dad had bought our house with a five-pound cash deposit, placed proudly on the counter of a local estate agent, we were moving to the adjacent Victorian part that had been created when Birmingham became a city.

Our suburban tree-lined road was one of the oldest in south Birmingham. It separated the frozen-in-time chocolate-box village from the sombre concrete shopping centres with their endless parades of women with pushchairs and old ladies in headscarves dragging their trolleys laden with convenience goods. Such shopping centres were everywhere in the 80s and were meant to promote postwar commercialism and forward thinking. In reality they were just concrete eyesores that we would be stuck with for a long time yet. These conflicting environments would be the backdrop to our childhood, grey and green playgrounds. We would grow to love what both sides represented: commercialism and the unbounded freedom of the outdoors.

Our road consisted of the once palatial, now forgotten homes of the Victorian nouveau riche, which were slowly being bulldozed back into the earth they sprang from and replaced with new, uniform estates which stood amongst the overgrown acres of abandoned gardens ready for new families to bring them to life. Our neat square of garden spilled downwards to the two things that remained defiantly untouched; the disused railway and the traditional red-brick school building with its separate entrances for boys and girls. As an adult I would lament upon the traditional old houses that were annihilated to make way for the repetitive yellow and red semis with integral garages and impractical conservatories. However, at four years old, as the remnants of the old order fell around me, I was oblivious as long as I could figure out how to coil my hair around my ears like Princess Leia, and there were plenty of places for Tony and me to explore. That was all that mattered.

We adapted very quickly to our new environment – first thing in the morning there was the predictable slow hum of the milk float and the clink of glass against glass as the milkman in his peaked cap and overall left our milk on the doorstep. If my parents weren't quick enough to wake up and bring the milk in the birds would beat them to it and peck off the foil bottle seals. Mid-morning, around twice a week, the rosy-faced baker in his white soufflé-shaped hat would ring the bell and we would rush to the door to eye up the huge basket of bread and cakes dangling over his arm. One day Mom answered the door to another person in fancy dress; a stern-looking lady all in black, except for her white apron and frilly cap. She carried a silver salver tray with cards. To our dismay there was no food but Mom became rather excited about the cards.

3

Apparently the elderly lady who lived in the big old house opposite ours had invited our parents to a drinks reception (this, we were told, was a grown-up word for a party). We weren't allowed to go but we whined and protested so much that Mom and Dad eventually reluctantly agreed to take us, as long as we kept quiet and didn't touch anything. Of course we planned to touch everything!

The day of the drinks reception/party came and disappointingly there was no pass the parcel, no balloons (not even a long wavy one or one in the shape of a sausage) – and quite frankly the host, in her bath chair and pearls, didn't look like she would survive a round of musical bumps, so Tony and I took the first chance we had and made a swift exit as soon as our parents were engrossed in one of their favourite topics: the wine.

When we had previously walked past this house and looked down its steep drive, as wide as a road, and up at the endless windows, and walls as tall as castle turrets, we had the feeling that if we were actually allowed to lie down and roll down that drive, we would roll directly into the past. We didn't of course, but we had great fun trying. After that we ran from room to room pressing the many buttons on the walls that sounded like bells. Tony said they would open trap doors but they didn't work, which must have been why the lady in the black and white outfit kept coming in to presumably fix them and we had to run off. We found the old lady's princess-style four-poster bed. She had an old photo of a man in a soldier's outfit next to it. Mom had told us the lady had never married and had no children so we reckoned she loved to play war games like we did. However, although Tony looked for ages we couldn't find so much as a cowboy's hat!

To round off our adventure we had a few goes at sliding

down the massive stairs. I laughed so much at the sight of Tony shouting and lying face down with his body bobbing on each bump until he skidded across the parquet floor at the bottom. By the time our parents had finished their 'drinks reception' and left the drawing room with what had to be the worst party bag filler ever (bunches of grapes from the vines in the host's conservatory) we were sitting cross-legged and quiet at the bottom of the stairs, too worn out from our expedition to do much else.

'What wonderfully well-mannered children you have!' the old lady exclaimed. Our parents naturally agreed. We allowed them to indulge in the delusion for a while until we had our bath later that night and Mom saw Tony's friction burns. He had to explain himself then and he got a right telling off! I didn't of course because I'd denied all knowledge of what he'd done. There was no evidence of me sliding down any stairs, besides I'd taken the smart approach and used a silver salver.

Very soon our house had been extended on Dad's modest salesman's salary and while digging the extensions the builders had uncovered a vast cellar that had never been properly filled in. I remember my parents, Tony and me all peering excitedly into the cavern from fifteen feet above and spying the Victorian furniture that had been hurriedly thrown down in the rush to get the modern homes erected. There was a brass bedstead, a walnut dresser, a cast iron range and various coloured mosaic tiles amongst masses of other dark wooden contraptions. My dad was quick to agree with the builders that it was a load of old-fashioned worthless junk and it would be quicker to just fill the lot in with lorry loads of cement rather than fish it out, so that is exactly what they did.

At the same time up and down the country, fellow builders

were ripping out unfashionable original features of Victorian homes, or turning them into bedsits at the eager requests of their owners, desperate to shake off the restrictions of the old world. No one with any sense of style or wealth would want to surround themselves with such old-fashioned things. Modernity, with its bright colours and prized objects, made possible by advances in man-made materials was the only way forward. It may be valuable and desirable now but back then Victorian original features and furniture were compulsively destroyed or concealed in favour of all things plastic, veneered, cheerful and bright.

It was hard to imagine the houses my grandparents' generation had grown up in, which they spoke of with great nostalgia, even though they had no inside bathrooms or radiators and only rich people had cars. I would often beg my Nanny Pearl and Grandad Jimmy to recite their tales of 'the olden days' like they were fiction and listen in awe to stories of the past where apparently 'everyone knew their place'.

We knew our parents were improving their social class ranking by the subtle signs in our environment. The dinner parties were the first clue, held for no apparent reason, where we would sit at the top of the stairs in our towelling pyjamas and hear the conversations of grown-ups wafting through the stippled glass dining room door. My dad would show off his extensive knowledge of wines and cheeses which were displayed during and after dinner. We didn't understand why the Blue Nun (German, ssh, don't tell Grandad) and Tiger Milk deserved a speech, nor why the empty bottle of Mateus Rosé in its straw coat and candle hat should haunt the dining room like some pointless souvenir for months after. For someone who had hardly been abroad you would be forgiven for thinking my dad was the proud owner of several European vineyards rather than a few products from aisle four at the Co-op. We just wanted them to stop banging on about the stinky mouldy cheeses, that looked like the stuffing we pulled out of the back of the sofa when we were bored, and talk about the type of subjects we were perched at the top of the stairs to overhear, such as how good Tony and I had been and what they had bought us for Christmas.

The other clues to our new upwardly mobile status were the household gadgets, arriving at regular intervals so that at one point, as you stumbled into the kitchen for breakfast, you would be forgiven for thinking you had somehow arrived at a house-warming party for appliances. Fondue anyone? The microwave was such a celebrity that my mother's friends came round especially to see it (along with the collection of microwave cookery books that graced every worktop). They were all in awe of the little box with the light and the plate that went round and round and promised to release housewives from the kitchen grindstone forever. Forget the coral earrings, the Janet Reger under-slips and the hostess trolley. On the top of my mother's friends' Christmas lists that year was a brown electric box that made cakes look anaemic while their owners pored over catalogues in search of the next kitchen revolution.

'Lazy, that's what that thing is!' declared Nanny Pearl as she gestured the steam iron towards it in indignation. 'That lovely pinny and matching oven gloves we bought your mother last Christmas, I suppose they'll have no use now,' she complained before turning her attention back to ironing socks. I looked up from my word search book and studied Grandad Jimmy who had come in from the garden and was standing quite still, silently regarding the plate in the miraculous brown box spin round and round.

'Grandad,' I whispered, 'Grandad, I think you are meant to put food in it first.' It was no good, he was in some sort of trance. After about twenty seconds he opened the microwave door, peered inside, and with a disheartened shrug of the shoulders walked slowly back outside.

Shortly after that my parents returned in high spirits to announce that they had put down a deposit on a dishwasher and Nanny Pearl's face looked as though they had announced the outbreak of World War III.

I decided to leave the strange disapproving atmosphere of the kitchen and go and find Tony. Maybe he would have some gun caps left we could use. I eventually found him standing on the ottoman with his head in the airing cupboard.

'Look, look!' he gestured, 'see what I found in here!' I put down my word search and climbed on top of the ottoman. I put my head in the stifling airing cupboard. The air was hot and dry from the water tank below and smelled of lavender and talc.

'There's nothing here except the ironing Tony.'

'No, look right at the back! I found pop! I found a secret supply of pop!'

Sure enough, behind the wall of neatly folded laundry, there were rubber tubes leading into some sort of glass container, and dripping into the container there was indeed some red coloured pop.

'Do you think it's Tizer?' said Tony almost salivating at the thought. We weren't allowed fizzy pop unless we went to someone's birthday party.

'No, I think it's cherryade,' I told him. 'Before they put the bubbles in. There's no way Mom could have noticed it's there.'

'Yes,' Tony agreed. 'She doesn't ever look at the back, she only ever puts the ironing in and then shouts at anyone that tries to get stuff out.'

I could feel the excitement rising inside me at this very important secret discovery.

'Tony, I really think that when this house was built they put this secret pop maker in for the children. There are so many things in this house for grown-ups, it makes sense that they should have made some for us too.'

'Do you really think so,' said Tony, his eyes wide and amazed. 'What about the bubbles though? You can't have cherryade without bubbles! How do the bubbles get in?' We stood there pondering the all-important question for a moment before having a eureka moment when we remembered something Dad had recently brought home for us for being so well behaved during the house move. Yet another guest at our kitchen gadget party, currently chilling out in a corner. We looked at each other and could hardly speak with excitement and the revelation except to declare, 'The SodaStream!'

Christmas was fast approaching and when Tony and I were sent to bed we could talk of nothing else. The presents, Nanny Pearl's notorious dinner and luxury buffets, the endless family tubs of Quality Street with no restrictions on the amount we could indulge in! When our parents became tired of the sound of our endless chatter floating down the stairs our father would threaten us with 'Wee Willie Winkie' from the nursery rhyme. Apparently he was the inappropriately clothed assistant of Father Christmas whose job it was to trawl the streets with his nightgown and candle looking for naughty children who wouldn't go to sleep, and reporting back to him so he could reduce the presents list.

We certainly didn't want to get caught out, but the thrill of Christmas was too much to lull us into tiredness so I would keep watch for Wee Willie out of the bedroom window while Tony made us some secret red pop with the SodaStream he had smuggled under the bed.

The pop was disgusting. It tasted like fizzy vinegar. The builders of our house had obviously given no thought at all to the recipe. Tony reckoned it must be the kind of pop that children drank in the olden days. As I was intrigued by anything people used to do in the olden days, thanks to my grandparents' stories and my Enid Blyton and Anne of Green Gables books, I blanked out my taste buds and drank it down in the dark. Not wanting to be outdone, Tony drank two cups.

We continued our Wee Willie Winkie vigil for a while after that, growing gradually more excitable about Christmas and more giggly, especially when Tony somehow managed to fall off his bed, head first into the toy box. He staggered out slowly, He-Man and Battle Cat attached comically by their body armour to his hair. I laughed hysterically and there was a final ultimatum shouted up the stairs: 'I said quiet you two! Wee Willie Winkie is outside!'

Tony and I looked at each other wide-eyed and in total horror. He was here! And we would get no presents. To the sound of much mutual 'shushing' we climbed carefully up to the window ledge and eased the zig-zag patterned curtains aside just enough to peep.

There he was! The man himself! Not clad in a dress and silly nightcap but a checked trouser suit, and holding a clipboard instead of a candle, but he was here and we had been rumbled. What's more he was walking down our driveway and about to ring the bell.

Then in an unusually bold move we had the compulsion to open the window and try to distract him.

'Psst Willie!' I hollered towards the porch

'Wee!' shouted Tony with the subtlety of a thunderclap.

The suited man looked up at us with a puzzled expression.

'Please Wee,' I shouted at him, feeing unusually confident. 'Please ask him if I can I have Star Wars figures and not girls' stuff, please please please!'

It was Tony's turn, 'Where are all the elves?' We both collapsed in peals of laughter. Immediately we heard the thundering sound of adult feet running up the stairs. That's when you know the shit's really about to go down. We ran for the cover of our beds; best pretend to be asleep.

Our dad burst into the room shouting something about how he and Mom would never be able to do the Pools again and how we had shown them both up. On went the light switch, up we both sat, bolt upright and protesting about being taken off Father Christmas's gift list while not comprehending why our dad was so hell bent on swimming.

We were so confused and panicky that I felt sick, I started to cry, Dad was shouting, Tony was wobbling on the side of his bed again and suddenly the remains of the strawberry Angel Delight we had had for pudding, combined with the olden days pop, spurted inconveniently from my mouth between sobs and landed in a neon pink puddle on my duvet.

The next day we saw our dad remove all the secret pop from the airing cupboard. He put it in a bottle and it went to live with the empty Mateus Rosé basket in the dining room so he could show it off at the next dinner party – which just proved that grown-ups knew absolutely nothing about what constitutes great food and drink.

Berni Inn

Nanny Pearl and Grandad Jimmy were obsessed with two things: home improvements and what they were having for dinner. Now that their children had long since left home and Grandad had worked his way up through British Gas, they were free to splurge their excess income on themselves and their stomachs. Long gone were the postwar hardships Nanny Pearl had told me about, when there was often nothing but bread and jam for dinner and when repairing the family shoes and clothes for one more winter was the norm. They had lost time and missed dreams to make up for and they intended to do it in style.

They used forty years' worth of meticulously 'set aside' savings and snapped up a large patch of clay soil in a land of mud and diggers. This was, our parents told us, Nanny and Grandad's new home as the six of us stood wellied up and squelching about in a field. It seemed a rather unusual choice to me, especially as Nanny was so house proud, but what did I know about the extremities of the adult brain?

'And this,' announced Grandad Jimmy, 'is the kitchen,' waving his arm across an expanse of wet mud which led to comments such as, 'Ooh it's a great size,' and, 'What a find, I bet you can't wait to move in!' I pondered for a moment upon the practicalities of my nanny's new life in the soil, as she had always seemed to live in the kitchen; baking, ironing and amassing vast quantities of packets of soap under the sink. She called it her 'stocks'. She must have been preparing for this clean-up job most of her adult life. Each to their own, I thought, and hoped that the adults would hurry up and stop gassing. If we didn't get back soon we would miss *Bullseye*.

By the time we returned to the site some months later it had been magically transformed into something more recognisable, a red brick maze of cul-de-sacs with our grandparents' new home somewhere amongst it. Inside was a vast expanse of brown, gold and tassels with a coal-effect fire with faux Victorian surround in the lounge, complete with faux brass coal scuttle and fireplace tools for filing and stoking the electric mock coals. Everywhere you looked there was a nod to the grand old days of the last century, from the port in the lead crystal decanter on display, to the huge eight-seater dining table with its Queen Anne legs. It was a contradiction in terms. On the one hand people were enthusiastically ripping out, boarding up, demolishing and burning anything from the days of the British Empire, while on the other they were spending a fortune replacing them with replicas.

'All you need to do is get a fine paintbrush and just touch up the fireplace detail in gold paint,' my dad was suggesting to Grandad Jimmy, as he opened up the giant mahogany globe on legs that doubled up as a secret bar (presumably to remind the adults of the places that they would love to visit if only those places were less 'foreign').

Well, there was no need to visit anywhere at all when they now had everything they ever wished for at their fingertips: comfort, luxury, gold tassels, and enough food to keep the conversation flowing between waking and sleeping. Even some of the walls and ceiling were turning into food. There was something called Aertex all over them, which resembled the top of the lemon meringue pies we used to get for pudding sometimes. Mom couldn't wait for us to be able to afford meringue walls too.

Nanny Pearl cooked properly. By properly I mean from scratch and without what she viewed as the 'lazy' methods the younger generation were getting accustomed to and having the nerve to call 'cooking'. 'Just add milk' powder sachets or instant microwave meals were the scourge of the devil. She did get a microwave for show at some point, or perhaps my parents or one of the aunts bought one for her, but it remained redundant for most of the decade. Years later she conceded that she might have used it, but she could never work out where to light it.

Her life seemed to be a endless whirlwind of peeling, chopping, stirring, and dishing up delicious meals on fancy plates. Then she and Grandad Jimmy would offer a critique on the offerings between mouthfuls before retiring to the kitchen to wash and dry up (by hand of course), sitting down for an hour or so and then getting up to start the whole process again. The result was that any visit to their home was comfort food heaven. Every meal was topped with lashings of homemade gravy or custard and there was always a home-baked cake in an old Quality Street tin available for a snack while you balanced your cup and saucer on your lap. Nanny Pearl liked nothing more than feeding everyone and reaping the compliments, and fishing for them if they weren't quickly forthcoming. 'How did you find the pastry? I used half butter, half margarine,' or 'Beryl over the road says my jam sponge is the best she's ever tasted, I steam it properly you know.'

The food at Nanny Pearl's was a far cry from what we were used to at home and school, which is probably why they never ate at our house despite being there frequently. The food we lived on at home was typical for an 80s kid. The popularity of the microwave was starting to change the way families ate. Around the same time, cheap convenience food was starting to flood the market and was snapped up by housewives, delighted about how much time and effort they could save. Why make a pie and pastry from scratch if you could buy them frozen? Faggots and concertina carrots? Yes please! The baby boomers had no desire to be chained to the kitchen like their mothers had been, so convenience food was a welcome invention. Only the Sunday roast was still a staple in many homes but foreign influences were starting to creep in as housewives experimented with different dishes. However, most of these efforts would not receive a pass mark if they were dished up today.

A school friend's mom used to make a 'signature' dish of spaghetti bolognese. The ingredients consisted of minced beef and onion mixed with tomato puree and a few diced carrots. Once drowned in dried mixed herbs and some pow-dered Parmesan cheese (that smelled like old socks) everyone declared it tasted just like what you would get in Italy! The funny thing was that no one had ever been to Italy, yet put a homemade spag bol in front of them and some people were miraculously transformed into restaurateurs. My parents, thankfully, did not show much interest in foreign cuisine. Their adventurous food night seemed to be limited to Fridays, when they often had their own private cheese and wine night with miniature cheeses from around Europe (Brie, Edam, Cheddar and the sausage-shaped one smelled of old socks).

My friend Ruth Payne's parents went a step further. They were already pushing the boundaries of culture and food in the 80s. They were embracing vegetarianism and even dabbling in veganism. It was at Ruth's house that I first tried carob as a chocolate substitute, vegetable lasagne and tofu. My mom was so fascinated by what they ate I was grilled constantly after I had visited there and it was a hot topic of conversation. At the school gates, all the mothers wanted to know how they were making all this stuff. Mr Payne was quite happy to give out the recipes as long as the mothers refused to buy anything South African due to apartheid.

For the average family like ours in the 80s, a meal out was reserved for special occasions or courting couples. Eating steak or scampi was considered a bit posh. When we were around eight years old Nanny Pearl and Grandad Jimmy announced, with all the pomp like we had just become next in line to the throne, that they were taking us out for a meal at the local Berni Inn. This was a definite mark of recognition of our increasing maturity as before this age we were undoubtedly considered too feral, with our fidgeting, constant interrupting and incessant nagging to try beer, wine and cigars. By the age of eight we could just about hold it together for an hour with the promise of an extra special pudding (sorry, I mean 'sweet') and total control of the after-dinner mints.

Special clothes were bought for the occasion. Much to my disgust it was compulsory that I would have to wear a 'pretty' skirt rather than my usual jeans and jumper ensembles, but I sucked it up rather than allow Tony to experience the majestic event without me.

Hair brushed to within an inch of its life and with a touch of mom's Avon blusher to add some colour to our cheeks we waited in the hall, trussed up like Christmas turkeys, for our grandparents' arrival in their Ford Sierra. I wasted no time in telling Tony that he looked like a total div in his trousers, waistcoat and bow tie, and I pressed my tongue into my lower jaw, gurn style, and flapped my hands up and down while chanting, 'Joey.' He retaliated by calling me a 'spaz' and a 'slap-head' while slapping his forehead with his palm repeatedly. It's probably his fault that I grew up with a complex about having a gigantic head.

We looked like butter wouldn't melt by the time our grandparents arrived and our parents waved us off proudly at the door as we embarked on our small trip into adult civilisation. The conversation coming from the driver and passenger seat on the way consisted of a long list of what they had indulged in during the many visits they had made to the Berni Inn and similar establishments. It was a non-stop dialogue of, 'You should try the smoked salmon,' with an air of importance and, 'Then they brought out the t-bone steak. You should have seen the size of it! Tell them about the gammon Jimmy!' They could have been talking about life on Mars for all we knew. Don't get me wrong, we were genuinely interested and excited about our excursion, but we were missing something. We just didn't get this level of exaltation over meals out that the adults around us clearly did. The older a person was, the more bizarrely they behaved when given the opportunity to indulge in food and be waited on. I mean, Tony was once was given two flakes in his Mr Whippy by accident and the excitement lasted for as many minutes, but really there must be more to life than food once you grew up.

Years later I realised that as most of our grandparents and some of our parents had experienced wartime rationing and genuine deprivation and hunger, food had become the holy grail. The excitement of a three-course meal, actually cooked and served to you and accessible to the average person was almost too much to entertain.

The Berni Inn attempted to replicate a Victorian grand interior with a dark mahogany effect bar, wooden tables, carpets of swirling yellows and browns on burgundy and matching padded, upholstered seats. We were shown to our tables by a uniformed waitress who called Grandad Jimmy, 'Sir,' and I swear Granddad's walk changed slightly and he strutted like a cockerel to the table which was laid with all manner of napkins, knives and forks in a row. We were fascinated and looked around. There were so many couples all dressed up here, mostly Grandad Jimmy and Nanny Pearl's age, with so many strings of pearls and silk handkerchiefs in suit pockets, they were impossible to count. There were a few young un-marrieds, that were probably dating, but mostly it was the same wartime generation, now approaching or beginning retirement, giving two fingers to their working-class roots, ecstatic that they could at last have a piece of what they could only have dreamed of when they were young.

First we had drinks brought to us: Campari and soda for our grandparents and Coke for us. This was a real treat as we only had Coke at birthday parties or when we were allowed to use the SodaStream. It had slices of lemon in it, which was a bit weird but we certainly weren't complaining. Next, we had something called a 'prawn cocktail' which looked like worms in blancmange but was quite nice. Grandad Jimmy recommended that we had steak with onion rings, mushrooms, chips and peppercorn sauce. We all had the same and Grandad gave us a running commentary on all the different types of steak and how he had sampled every one. If there had been a TV show called 'Steak Off' back in the 80s, I swear Grandad Jimmy would have starred in it. The best bit, and the bit that we were looking forward to the most, was the 'sweet', or pudding as it was known in common circles. To be honest we were pretty stuffed and our backsides were numb due to all the sitting still listening to food lectures by then, but it was a crime for a child to refuse anything with sugar so we went for the ice cream sundaes, complete with fan-shaped wafers that made them taste better. Grandad and Nanny opted for the Black Forest gateau. To our astonishment they then requested a cheese board and coffee which was served along with grapes and After Eight mints.

I am still baffled at the 1980s need to wash down a bottle of wine with coffee and cheese. The craze seems to have fallen out of favour and I'm glad. It seemed like a perfectly good way to ruin a fun time. It was as though the moral police would storm the steak houses up and down the country shouting, 'Stop drinking now people!' 'Put that wine glass down and get yourself a strong coffee in case you get drunk!' 'Here, eat this Brie, this should detract from the taste of lager!' Incidently, I don't remember binge drinking being a popular pastime in the 80s, nor getting drunk for fun. Perhaps those cheese boards really did keep everyone in check back then. Once they went out of fashion no one knew when to stop.

Although Tony and I went to a Catholic primary school we rarely went to church on a Sunday. We usually spent the Lord's special day at our grandparent's posh new house enjoying a full on Sunday roast-followed by something covered in custard or a home-made lemon meringue pie. Our religion was a

Sunday roast in the brown and gold tasselled palace, the Top 40 Countdown, and then *Bullseye* in that order. Jesus would have loved it I reckon.

Tony and I loved Sundays afternoons as we could take our ghetto blasters to our grandparents' house and listen to the Top 40 on the radio, even if this did involve the inconvenient echo of Grandad Jimmy in the background commenting on how, 'This isn't music'. We used to laugh and ignore him as he babbled on about someone called Sinatra who knew how to sing. Way before we were allowed to venture without a parent into our local Woolworths to splurge our pocket money on records we discovered the delights of making our own Top 40 mix tapes. It was so simple and cost nothing. All you needed to do was listen to the Top 40 Sunday countdown and wait for the DJ to announce your favourite chart songs, then, provided you were quick with your reflexes and could hit the record button in the split second before he stopped talking and the music started, you could build yourself your perfect mix tape. This could then be played repeatedly after school for weeks (or at least until the cassette ribbon got chewed up by the ghetto blaster and all attempts to salvage it by winding it back in with a pencil failed). The only problem with this was that you never knew what order your desired song would be played in and there was no catch up option so if you needed the loo or you were called down for tea at an inopportune moment and you missed your song, tough. You had lost your chance until the following Sunday.

Bullseye was a great show. It was where ordinary people had a darts competition and could win incredible prizes; mostly they were the home gadgets and furnishings that everyone was lusting after at the time. If the contestants got through

21

to the final then they could gamble all their prizes away in order to win 'Bully's Special Prize'. Every viewer and the audience wanted them to gamble and would shout advice at them, even through the TV screen. If they gambled and won, everyone could get ridiculously excited over the special prize of a speedboat or a caravan, which would slide out from behind a screen or get pushed to the forefront of a studio by TV crew dressed like barber shop signs, all red and white stripes and grins.

Everyone wondered how Barry from Birmingham and his mate Dave managed to store or use that speedboat when they lived so far away from a coast or lake. I can tell you the answer to this one as one of our neighbours actually bought that *Bullseye* speedboat from one of the show winners and had it on his driveway between 1980 and 1989; it didn't move throughout that whole time. The nearest our neighbour had ever been to sailing was one time when he took his dingy out in Weston-super-Mare and it got wedged between a sand shelf and a load of old tyres. It didn't matter. The speedboat was the ultimate success symbol, whether it was on a driveway or moored on a lake. Whether you could actually drive one wasn't important so our neighbour made use of it the best he could. In the summer he used to grow rhubarb in it and my mom and Nanny Pearl used to make the most incredible crumble from it. Who needed a *Miami Vice* lifestyle anyway when you could watch it on TV from the comfort of your own home?

'Can He Eat Crisps?'

Tony and I started primary school in 1980. St Anthony's was an imposing Victorian red-brick building, surrounded by spiked, wrought iron, railings painted green. This type of school is generally extinct today, due to health and safety, but in the early 1980s most cities and towns still had an abundance of them.

There were two playgrounds, one for boys and one for girls separated by more spiked railings. There was one 'temporary' Portakabin classroom for the infants that had been there for the last twenty years. They were lucky because they had indoor toilets; the only toilets for the older kids were in a dark brick built hut in the playground and needing to go was not a straightforward experience. The only light was from slits high up in the walls so it was like entering a cavern which stank of urine no matter what time you went in. Getting to your desired location meant negotiating suspicious-looking puddles, pink carbolic soap that was always cracked with black paint, and an explosion of scrunched-up paper towels and greaseproof toilet roll. On arrival at your location, achieving privacy meant closing the cubicle door and sitting in pitch darkness. Sometimes it was easier not to bother. Constipation rates amongst children in the 80s were high. Experts blamed ignorant diets. I blame school toilets. There was one kid, who shall remain anonymous, who would offer to wash the paintbrushes and then take a dump in the cloakroom sink. The teachers would label it sinful and lazy, but perhaps he was just thinking outside the box.

On our first day we stood like a pair of circus show freaks in front of our classroom and were introduced to our peers by a kindly young teacher called Miss McCoughney with Lady Diana hair and baby blue eyeliner. We could hear the loud excited whispers of 'twins!' and twenty-seven pairs of expectant eyes fixed upon us as if awaiting for us to put on some sort of show. As the new kids we were the centre of attention, like mini celebrities. Everyone wanted to hang out with us until the novelty wore off about a week later when we were no longer new kids but two standard St Anthony's pupils. However, our celebrity status that first day was nothing in comparison to the memorable introduction of one new kid, a few years later, who reduced our entire class to a fascinated and open-mouthed silence.

He was different to anyone else most of the children had ever seen and he looked as nervous as our teacher did as he shuffled from one foot to another and looked at the floor.

'This is Yaw,' said Mr Proud our headteacher, smiling over him like Jesus, with his hands on his shoulders. 'He is joining Junior Two and I am sure you will all make him feel very welcome.' He then made a rapid exit and left the visibly nervous Miss McCoughney, to face the barrage of questions. Loud whispers flew around the class. 'He's black! He's black!'

'Where's he from Miss?'

'Why don't you ask him yourself, Damien?'

'Where you from, Yaw?'

'Cotteridge,' said Yaw very quietly. Damien's brow crinkled in puzzlement as he tried to work it out

'Cotteridge as in down the road or Cotteridge as in Africa?'

I was as puzzled as everyone else. Surely if there was a black family living down the road then someone would have noticed this phenomenon and reported excitedly back to the rest of the community. It was like the time I had seen that punk rocker with the green spiky hair and the safety pin through his nose exiting Braggs the Bakers, munching on a sausage roll, although I'm not sure anyone believed me.

My friend Ruth, who was something of a child genius due to having two parents who were university professors and free-thinking liberals confidently put up her hand.

'There is no Cotteridge in Africa and Yaw is probably as English as we are. In fact, his grandparents probably came to England in the 1950s to help with a shortage in the labour market. My father lectures in social and economic history and that's how I know.'

Yaw looked up at her amazed.

'My dad is a teacher at the university too! He teaches English.' He then sunk back embarrassed at his desk as he noticed the entire class silently staring at him open mouthed like goldfish. It was quite incredible. A black family with an eight-year-old boy whose father was a teacher, and no one had noticed or mentioned it before today! Miss McCoughney swallowed quickly and shot a relieved look at Ruth. 'Right children!' She snapped into teacher mode and wrote the date on the blackboard. 'Time to start today's work.'

The morning passed uneventfully and included soaking card and coloured tissue paper in Copydex and satisfyingly peeling the plastic remnants off our fingers. By breaktime we had far more exciting and pressing matters to attend to. A few of us located Yaw quietly playing with a tennis ball in the blocked-up doorway of the former air raid shelter in the playground. We simply had to know more. Within minutes he was cornered. Even Mark Walton and his band of 'thickie' friends who followed him everywhere stopped their game of superheroes and galloped over, duffel coats tied around their necks like capes flapping in the wind. We watched Yaw in wonder, willing him to do something to break the ice, but he didn't, he just froze. Eventually one of the thickie gang piped up, 'Can he eat crisps?'

Slowly, several bags of Fish 'n' Chips, Piglets and pickled onion Monster Munch were proffered. Yaw accepted a selection. 'Look at his hands,' said someone. His palms were lighter than the rest of his skin.

'Oh that's because when God sprayed him brown he must have had his hands on the wall and he missed a bit. Fancy not knowing that,' said Caroline Harper, hands on hips, as she liked to appear knowledgeable about everything to do with God.

'For goodness' sake,'exclaimed Ruth. 'You are so stupid! God doesn't walk around with aerosol cans! Come on Yaw!' she said and stomped off. Yaw followed her along with myself, Colleen Fahey and Jennifer Bryan trailing behind. I adored Ruth. She wasn't scared to be different.

'What are you looking at pancake boobies?' Colleen shouted back at Caroline. 'Shrove Tuesday isn't for ages yet!' Her three older brothers had taught her to be queen of the put-down. Caroline let out a dramatic sob, and ran off to cry in the corner, followed by most of our class (including Matthew Connelly who had been winking at me all morning, making me suddenly conscious of my hair). We didn't care. We had the interesting new boy in *our* gang.

Back then neither me nor my suburban-raised 1980s col-
leagues had ever seen anyone that wasn't a shade of snowy
white outside of the odd corner shop in real life. Ignorance
prevailed amongst younger adults and anyone who hadn't
served abroad in the Second World War. The truth was most
suburban adults had never ventured outside of Britain. But
it wasn't only people of colour that were regarded with both
fascination and trepidation; for the first ten years of my life
I thought that French children ate frogs' legs and snails for
breakfast. I reckon it was partly Miss McCoughney's fault.
Once, when it was our class's turn to do an assembly, the theme
was, 'Children of Europe,' I was given the part of the French kid
'Pierre'. I was told to ride around the stage in a striped t-shirt
and beret with a string of garlic round my neck shouting, 'Ooh
la la!' while the kid from Holland picked tulips and lived in a
windmill and the Italian sold Cornettos rather than going to
school. Thankfully, there wasn't a German kid simultaneously
goose-stepping across the stage.

The English working classes believed they knew everything
about the world and its cultures without setting foot on foreign
soil. For that reason, any non-British child was regarded as
both a celebrity and a reason to be cautious. It was something
of a surprise the first time Mrs Oworae, Yaw's mother, turned
up at the school gates, not in full African dress and a zebra on
a lead as some then may have expected, but in a floaty Laura
Ashley dress, fitted coat and expensive handbag that the other
mothers envied. She told them that her husband gave her an
allowance each month to keep herself looking nice, causing a
few of the mothers to look like they had been slapped round
the face with a copy of *Woman's Weekly*.

On the way home, after our routine stop at the sweet shop on the corner for a bag of ten-pence mix, I chatted excitedly to our mother about Yaw, the latest new kid, in between mouthfuls of cola bottles and white mice. Tony was banging on about his best mate Brian King. From what I had already seen of him I couldn't stand Brian King. He was a spoilt brat who was given all the best parts in the school plays just because his mom went to church every Sunday and helped run the school craft club. According to Tony, Brian had every Star Wars toy and gadget in existence. Brian said his dad was an astronaut and had brought him back a piece of rock from Pluto. He had let Tony borrow it and for a whole week Tony gazed in awe at a pumice stone on his bedside table before going to bed. I, of course, vowed to always have much more interesting and genuine friends. Ruth was my best friend and I used to nag my mom to speak to her dad so I could go to tea as often as possible.

Feminism in the 1980s; Still an Awfully Long Way to Go

I loved going to Ruth's house. Her mother was a rare specimen as she actually had a career. She was a university lecturer and something called a feminist and we didn't see much of her unless she was organising a CND march, when she gave us lots of badges to plaster all over our coats. Ruth's father was a professor and novelist who spent most of his time in his study, emerging only to go on school runs and cook weird and wonderful creations from far flung corners of the globe for us to sample. No microwaved pies or faggots in that house. We had the run of the dusty bohemian Victorian villa with its endless rooms full of books. To my mother's bemusement I would come back with tales of sampling stir-fried vegetables with tofu and vegan lasagne. She used to laugh like I'd announced we had dined on Play-Doh and wood shavings. She couldn't get over Mr Payne. 'Poor Mr Payne,' she used to say as he turned up in his creased overcoat, the only man on the school run. 'Imagine him having to iron his own clothes.'

We had encountered Ruth's mother, Celia Payne, once before in Cotteridge when we had been accompanying my mom and

Nanny Pearl to the shops to buy food for our Royal wedding street party. She was sitting at a desk outside Woolworths with a gang of people who looked like librarians. Surrounding her were photographs of burning cars, people fighting policemen, and people looking sad in bedrooms with only mattresses and no bedsheets. She tried to get Nanny to sign a petition to stop people celebrating the Royal wedding! Nanny Pearl's face looked as fierce as that time Tony put black pudding in her purse and she tried to pay for a cup of tea with it. She put her hands over our ears and marched us away with a disapproving pursed mouth. My mom later laughed about it with my dad. My grandparents' love of the Royal family was so great that any criticism of Her Majesty or any of her offspring was akin to blasphemy. My parents had no particular allegiance to them but my mom did love Lady Diana, and was always interested to see what she was wearing. Celia Payne's pursuit of social equality and refusal to look after her husband's stomach or wardrobe bemused my mother. Why try to overturn the way things had always been?

The subject of Prince Charles and Lady Diana's wedding was everywhere you went. In school, encouraged by Mr Proud, another staunch monarchist, we made a huge frieze with red, white and blue scrunched-up tissue paper and distorted drawings of the royal couple with Prince Charles's ears looking like he was about to take off. It was displayed outside our school gates. The mothers speculated on what 'Shy Di' would wear on the big day. Ruth's loyalties were torn and she joked about the poor taxpayers having to pay for Lady Diana's wedding dress, or 'tent' as she referred to it, but she happily joined in with the talk and excitement of the street parties that all children were attending. I wondered if her mother would have the heart to stop her from attending one. I was relieved in the end when, as a compromise, Ruth was allowed to sleep over at ours for the occasion. Ruth's mother put in a rare appearance the next day to pick her up and my mother asked her if she wanted a cup of tea. It was the first time they had properly met. They were poles apart and probably should not have got on at all but quite the opposite happened.

They chatted their way into the kitchen, my mom in her floral pinny and fur-accented slippers, Celia Payne in beaded jewellery, flowing scarves and tie dye harem pants. I don't think my mom had ever encountered someone like her before. She had plenty of mom friends at the school gate but the vast majority of them hadn't worked in any capacity since getting married. There seemed no need to. Husbands provided, wives stayed at home, had babies, fed everyone, cleaned up after their brood (got an allowance for themselves if they were lucky) and that was how it had always been. The concept of a wife and mother going out to work because they actually wanted to retain their independence was still quite unique.

Tony and I played close by the chatting mothers. Today, Tony was Darth Vader, I was Princess Leia and Ruth had insisted on being Han Solo. We could have played somewhere else but it was always good to multi-task playing and eavesdropping. We could hear my mother lamenting on having to leave grammar school at sixteen, followed by Celia saying something about the Open University, something about a school that only opened when it got dark, and something about feminism.

There was a magical aura around Celia Payne. Apart from her frustrations with social injustice and nuclear power she seemed to shine with life and possibilities rather than exist within the constraints of social expectation. She was like a visitor from the future. She didn't care about her house being pristine or what visitors might think, she had opinions, real opinions beyond who shot J R Ewing and a husband that encouraged them. She took her family on holiday to gîtes in rural France where they immersed themselves in the culture and she didn't care what anyone in their Butlin's chalet or Aberystwyth caravans thought about it. She was closer to the future and the 'space age,' than anyone I knew or had read about and I longed for her to adopt me. Ruth always said she was going to sort it and it wouldn't be a problem. I often tried to catch her mother's eye to see if I could glean a clue as to when I could be her new daughter, but Celia gave nothing away.

Shortly after Celia's visit and pep talk Mom enrolled in the mysterious night school to do A levels and my dad started swearing at the iron on a regular basis as he did battle with his shirts. I used to look around and wonder about this mysterious night school where the children and teachers only came out in the dark. Playtime must have been challenging but Mom seemed to be very excited about it. My dad wasn't so excited. It took him a few weeks weeks of walking around like a creased-up tramp before he figured out how to switch the iron on.

The moms at the school gates all looked like prematurely middle-aged women even though they were probably in their twenties and early thirties. They lapped up this talk of night school and feminism, like Mom was giving Jesus's sermon on the mount. The moms wore no make-up, their hair was short and permed and they wore A line skirts below the knee, matched with heavy cardigans in winter. Fashion in the 80s, it seems, catered for teenagers and unmarrieds in their early twenties. It was all snow-washed jeans, brightly coloured tops, plastic jewellery and stilettos; a look that we as children aspired to very much. Then there was a gaping fashion chasm for anyone between twenty and sixty and then there were the type of shops that Nanny Pearl would take us to on a Saturday when she was looking for a smart blouse or some monogrammed handkerchiefs. The anorak section of C&A was about as inspirational as a recorder performance at school but fortunately the cake stop at Druckers afterwards more than made up for it. Fashion for the young marrieds, however, was merciless.

With the exception of Princess Diana, a woman's wedding day was the last chance she had to wear anything nice. The day after her nuptials she generally woke up to find her wardrobe had been magically transformed by the moral police. Mom actually had a huge Aran cardigan knitted in a rust-coloured wool with flecks of white. It was like cuddling up to a tin of corned beef. Somewhere in the depths of her wardrobe were remnants of her 1960s and 70s pre-marriage clothes: heels that made a delightful clop-clop-clopping sound, mini skirts and skin-tight flares and hairpieces like Priscilla Presley. They were incredible to dress up in and such a contrast to what she wore now that I vowed that if I had to make such fashion compromises then I would never get married. Even though Matthew Connelly had promised me that if he got a ring in his Christmas cracker this year I could have it, a tempting offer, just so long as I could wear stilettos, huge neck bows and big hair, every day for the whole of my adult life.

I don't know why the non-career women in the 80s felt it necessary to dress in the same way that their mothers did. It was like marriage and motherhood came at the price of being invisible. Husbands and children were at the forefront of the happy domestic dream, wives lagging in the background, beige-clad and inconspicuous: keeping an immaculate home, full of the latest gadgets and luxuries but most of the time it was a mask. For many wives the mask would inevitably begin to slide one day, once the gadgets were past their best and the children had flown the nest, but right then, at the dawn of the 80s any dissatisfaction was nothing but a simmer below the surface of the nuclear family, easy to smooth over with a good episode of *Dallas* or the latest Kays catalogue.

Talking of catalogues and my mother's recent lecture on feminism, I decided it was time to take the bull by the horns and voice a feminist concern of my own. After spending literally hours of our spare time poring over heavy catalogues and circling everything we wanted for Christmas (which in Tony's case seemed to be followed up by a lengthy and inexplicable browse of the lingerie sections) the time had come for me to be direct and assertive.

Christmas was a challenge. I wanted Star Wars figures, but when I mentioned this to any family members who enquired, I got snorts of indignation

'You can't have Star Wars figures, what do you really want?'

What I really wanted could not be bought from shops. I wanted a time machine to transport me to the nineteenth century where I could float about in ballgowns and be waited on all day. I wanted my parents to fund my education at Malory Towers boarding school, I wanted to audition for the Royal Ballet School and be discovered as the twentieth-century answer to Anna Pavlova, despite never having had a ballet lesson, but as these things were not likely to happen I wanted Star Wars figures. Everyone had said no and I felt they were mocking me.

'Why can't I have Star Wars figures?' I pleaded with my

mother who was busy drinking tea with Nanny Pearl and listening enthusiastically while Grandad Jimmy held court on the merits of something called a Betamax and VHS. These were obviously the adult equivalent of Star Wars figures because none of them was actually listening to me. 'I want Star Wars figures like Tony. It's not fair. Why is he allowed to have Star Wars stuff and I can't have any? I only want Star Wars figures, that's all I want, Star Wars, why can't I have Star Wars?' All three of them momentarily stopped the cool adult gadget debate and said in unison, 'Because you're a girl!' before turning their attention back to what was obviously their own Christmas list. As I sulked my way out of the kitchen I spotted my mother actually getting the Kays catalogue out so they could look for VH Maxes or whatever they were. Sometimes I felt like all children were just there to be seen and not heard, unless there was a school assembly or a nativity going on.

I left the kitchen dejected and frustrated. It was 1980 not 1880 and yet I was being ridiculed and patronised for wanting to play with something that was cool rather than pretty. Celia Payne was right when she said there was something called first-wave feminism at the turn of the century when women wanted to vote, there was second-wave feminism in the 60s when women burned their bras (they shouldn't have bothered, they should have saved them all up and given them to Tony as Christmas presents, could have saved our parents a fortune) and now there was third-wave feminism and this must mean that girls could own Star Wars figures if they wanted to. There certainly was a long way to go!

'Proper Winters'

The days were getting colder and colder, which only meant one thing: Christmas was approaching. We awoke to giant icicles hanging like stalactites off the guttering outside our bedroom window and our mother mopping condensation puddles off the inside. We had thin radiators to heat our rooms but the impact wasn't warm and cosy, like it is today, because you had to lean against them to get dressed, which only resulted in a burned backside. When the heating was off (which was often, as it was so expensive,) you could make small clouds of fog by breathing out and simultaneously pretending to 'smoke' a pencil.

On the coldest mornings while we were putting our school uniforms on, a hot air blowy heater was set up on the floor. When you plugged it in it would emit a constant blast of hot air right at you. This also burned you if you got too close so it was better to grab a hairbrush and mirror, position yourself about five feet away from it and belt out a pop song through your windswept hair while you featured in your own pop video. Tony liked to sing 'Uptown Girl'. I preferred Andrew Lloyd Webber numbers (I was a bit weird like that), which resulted in much pounding of sock footballs to my head and shouts of,

'Shut up you idiot, you sound like a cat being strangled,' and I would retort, 'Look there's a woman coming down the road who looks just like Christie Brinkley,' so he would rush to the window in earnest anticipation. I would finish my rendition, while he searched excitedly for a supermodel who had got up that morning and thought, 'I'll just cancel the flight to Milan today, because I really fancy hooking up with a seven-year-old boy whose talents include wearing his father's bodybuilding chest expanders while brandishing a fish slice and shouting, 'By the power of Grayskull!'

One year it snowed so hard in December I thought it would never stop. At first, the snow was just a dusting. It was enough for us to make lethal slides of black ice in the playground that we had great fun skidding along and bouncing off when we lost our balance. Most kids in that decade had a good collection of scabs on their knees like badges of honour. You don't see this any more because schools are too frightened of being sued for negligence. Back then, if you suffered a cut knee from deliberately skidding on ice or a snowball in the eye it was your own fault, not the local authority's. Snowball fights were compulsory between the iron railings separating the girls' playground from the boys'. If you didn't want to join in you just chose to play somewhere else. If you took part it was at your own peril but, what the hell, it was fantastic, even when the ice on your woollen gloves meant that you couldn't feel your fingers and your rubber wellies made you feel like there were ice cubes between your toes.

As the snowfall intensified we would excitedly listen to the kitchen radio for our local station, BRMB, to announce that our school was closed due to the weather. If we heard nothing we trudged to school anyway, calf deep in snow, and if we were really lucky we would arrive just in time to see Mr Proud erecting a blackboard outside the school to let everyone know that school was closing due to frozen water pipes. I cannot exaggerate the sheer jubilation of that situation. Imagine arriving at work one day to be greeted by your boss telling you to take the day off to indulge yourself exactly as you please. You certainly wouldn't be taking to social media to complain and moan about how unfair it was that you actually had to travel into work and your hands were cold, and does anyone know what your legal rights are as to your wasted half an hour? No, you would be running out of that office in glee thinking about shopping, lunching, leisure pursuits, trashy daytime TV from the comfort of your lovely bed.

Our alternative day would start by us cheering loudly before racing home to make as much chaos in the snow-filled garden as we could muster. We'd make sculptures of men in woolly hats with carrot noses, igloos, and snowballs bigger than ourselves that would linger in the garden for weeks afterwards when everything had returned to green. Then we would go inside, usually when it was getting dark, and gaze in wonder at the strangely lit sky, the self-designed sculptures and what was left of the snow, now mashed into dirty squashed sludge. The best thing was that the next day the pure white stuff would be back and we could start all over again.

Christmas morning usually dawned like any other. In the weeks leading up to it the advent calendar doors had all been opened to show their surprise pictures of angels, candles and boxes tied up with pretty bows. This was before all the Christmas artists retired and someone with no imagination had decided to fill all advent calendars with chocolates. All previous Christmas list angst was forgotten as Tony and I raced downstairs in our towelling PJs at breakneck speed. It was still dark. It was probably before the time we struggled to get out of bed for school. Our parents, sensing the commotion, were no doubt fumbling for their dressing gowns half asleep.

The lounge was in darkness and when we turned on the light we saw the magic. Overnight our lounge had been turned into an Aladdin's cave. There were red, gold and green paper packages having a scrum on every conceivable surface. Foil decorations and cards with traditional snowy scenes were strung across the room like washing lines. We dashed in and ran amongst the packages screaming, 'Where's mine' 'Where's mine?' 'No' 'No.' 'No.' 'Here!' before claiming our own individual pile of gifts. Neither of us believed in Santa of course, not since we were four anyway. We would have loved to though and we were automatically swept up in the annual excitement as we put on a good show of gullibility for the adults. However, in reality, by the age of eight Santa's status as a man of magical powers, rivalled only by Jesus, was in the same category as ghosts. We would have loved to believe and we looked for proof regularly but so far we had found nothing conclusive. I watched Tony open his Millennium Falcon, AT-AT and Star Wars figure menagerie with a forced smile. My presents were lovely too but reeked of, 'we didn't know what to get her as she's not a normal girl.' There were, amongst the Yardley toiletries and books, novelty rubbers to add to my prized collection; rubbers in the shape of huge dice, ice creams and cartoon characters.

There was also always a selection box which would be de-voured before breakfast. All of my family had monogrammed handkerchiefs. What was it about the 80s and monogrammed handkerchiefs? Who on earth was in charge of that marketing ploy? How did they do it? What did a generation of people want with storing the contents of their snotty winter nostrils on a rag up their sleeve? Quite a lot apparently. They seemed to be the Christmas gift for anyone that was clueless as to what to buy for that tricky relative in the days before Argos vouchers. I've never seen them for sale since that decade but I reckon they are haunting the backs of cupboards somewhere waiting to make a comeback.

A close second to the monogrammed hankies in the 'I didn't know what to buy them' category was the soap-on-a-rope. Who on earth bathed in water so filthy and dark that they needed to harpoon their soap to a length of rope? Most of the adult male population it seemed, as this was almost exclusively a man's gift. My dad always seemed to get one. The soaps would live in bathrooms up and down the country for the next year, jostling for position amongst pumice stones, loofahs and scented talc and other now extinct bathroom 'must-haves'.

I was grateful to the person responsible for gifting me a solitary Princess Leia figure. It still stands out as a bittersweet memory; a testament to the final days when most women were still expected to know their place. It was OK though as Tony's Star Wars collection was going to be a free-for-all anyway.

I could actually boast of a present that would make Tony jealous because I got a Mr Frosty and he didn't. However, in spite of Mr Frosty's hype he did turn out to be a bit of an anti-climax. For all the time involved in making that plastic snowman and his YTS penguin mate produce a miniscule ice lolly you could have defrosted the freezer, squirted a load of cordial on top of the mess and stuck your head in it. It was OK though as just owning one of those items meant that all your mates wanted to come round and have a go.

I felt luckier than the vast majority of my Catholic school friends as we were not made to sit through church on Christmas morning before opening our presents, nor were we made to sit through midnight mass on Christmas Eve. We could just wake up and get stuck in. The truth was, although we went to a Catholic school, our lapsed Catholic parents rarely went to church. We were only at St Anthony's for 'the discipline,' We were plastic Catholics. It took me many years to realise that this was the reason I never was made a prefect, a head girl or got any decent parts in the school plays. In spite of my hard efforts at academia and good behaviour, which far outshone some of my fellow Catholic classmates, those important roles were strictly for those children who went to church on Sundays. Nepotism, within God's family, it seemed, was at play even during those early days.

After breakfast we went to Nanny Pearl and Grandad Jimmy's to congregate with cousins, uncles, aunts and neighbours. Dinner was an extravagant affair with never-ending portions. To this day I have never tasted comfort food quite as delicious as that conjured up by Nanny Pearl in that decade.

Absolutely everything would be homemade, in excess, and nothing was too much trouble. I knew just how Henry VIII must have felt at a feast. All of us grandchildren even had little tankards with our names engraved on them. We would then waddle into the lounge and share a tub of Quality Street in front of the TV and the Christmas special programmes which had been enthusiastically pre-selected and circled by the adults in the *Radio* and *TV Times*. Once the mountains of washing and drying up were finished, Nanny Pearl would suddenly conjure up High Tea with trifles, cold meats, salads, pickled onions, fondant fancies, mince pies and cake just in case we planned

41

to hibernate for the winter and build up our fat stores until spring.

After dinner the adults would finish off the wine and Tony and I would share a four-pack of Babycham served in cocktail glasses with glacé cherries and an umbrella. This was a special treat as no one seemed to believe that Babycham with the cute little deer on the bottle was real alcohol, more a special type of Christmas pop. Later, Grandad Jimmy would bang on about his time in the army until Nanny Pearl became irritated and told him to stop showing off, but not before he insisted on standing during the Queen's speech, much to our bemusement.

We were put to bed at the same time as all of our little cousins so that the adults could stay up, drink more wine and talk. The beds were super soft and smelled of fabric conditioner. It was like falling into a giant flannelette marshmallow. The layers of striped sheets and fleece blankets were tucked in so tight that if you rolled out you could lie suspended in a makeshift hammock. The following morning, after tiptoeing round the various unmarried uncles who littered the floor in put-up beds, it would be time for a cooked breakfast, with no elbows on the table. Generous helpings of the butcher's best sausages, bacon and black pudding accompanied by plenty of fried bread, eggs and grilled tomatoes. We had to request Nanny Pearl's permission to leave with a, 'Please may I leave the table?' and she would reply, 'Yes you may.' We would be itching to go off and explore on our bikes, which were kept there just for us.

Off we went, completely unsupervised, down the modern cul-de-sac and into the vast woods for miles and miles, along with the hordes of other local children on bikes, with not a care in the world. When we became hungry we would always find our way back for bubble and squeak made with yesterday's leftovers and not one of the adults was remotely concerned that we hadn't been seen for hours.

School Days

The first Amstrad computer graced our classroom in 1984 and this provided us with a classic teacher pranking activity that Tony must be given all the credit for. It was the only one in the school for as long as I was there and every class took their turn playing host to it. It was *very* exciting. A machine that interacted with you without any exchange of food or judgement was even more exciting than a new kid. There was only one game on it at first and it was a times tables quiz game. When it was your turn you had to enter your first name and then when you were asked a question the computer would say, 'Well done!' or, 'Wrong, never mind,' followed by your name. We couldn't get over how familiar the grey box in the corner was with us! Tony had the brainwave of entering his name as, 'Now sod off!' which was hilarious as the computer began to swear at you each time you answered a question. It took a few days for the teachers to discover the real reason why so many kids were suddenly so keen on learning their times tables. It took another few days for them to work out how to stop the swearing. However, most of us had learned them inside out by then.

Every spring term we returned to St Anthony's with football and Garbage Pail Kids stickers and obligatory collectors albums. Our pencil cases would also be fit to burst with novelty rubbers. In playgrounds up and down the country there were kids acting like enthusiastic car booters, comparing, adoring and bribing each other for their goods while they competed to become the best hoarder of novelty commercial items. We were no different. At home in our bedrooms line upon line of similar toys were showcased on shelves as we proudly assembled entire collections. Tony had several shelves of Star Wars figures which stood shoulder to shoulder. Most of the girls had gangs of My Little Ponies or Care Bears. It was the decade of collecting things. Celia Payne, despite her dislike of commercialism, relented once and bought Ruth some Star Wars figures for Christmas. It was like winning the lottery. We were girls but even so, between us we had amassed a total of five Star Wars figures! They were our 'collection'. We were mocked by the boys who said, 'Girls can't play with those!' and some of the girls were open-mouthed with shock as we flaunted Darth Vader and his stormtroopers at breaktime. The 'popular' girls, Caroline and Lisa, who liked to pretend that they were eighteen and only collected eyeshadow, said we were weird, but we didn't care. According to them, their mothers allowed them to spend their free time dancing manically to Duran Duran in ra-ra skirts and smoking pretend cigarettes made from rolled-up card and talcum powder (when you blew through them it sent a cloud of talc out that looked like real smoke, which apparently attracted boys). Ruth and I fantasised about obliterating them with light-sabers.

Mr Proud was terrifying as he towered before us each morning in assembly. This took place in a rickety corrugated tin tabernacle at the side of the school that at one time had served as a church. These days it would never have got through health and safety but back then it served us for assemblies, P.E.,school dinners and the dreaded end of year tests. He was actually a jovial man with a talent for telling bad jokes, and an immense pride in his school and all his pupils. However, his previous career as an Army major, combined with his broad shoulders, height of six foot four, and fierce 1950s values made him a terrifying prospect for the children, the teachers and the mothers. Even being selected for 'good work' sweets on a Friday and having to line up outside his office for them made us feel a strange combination of delight and fear. In Mr Proud's school naughty pupils would not be tolerated, naughty pupils like that Kevin who stole the Mars bar from the tuck shop were never seen again. So we knew that as long as we didn't step out of line Mr Proud would always have our backs.

Every assembly Mr Proud would tell a little story with a moral. The one I remember the most was that everyone God put on the Earth had a special talent. He told us about a former pupil who was never any good at lessons and used to run away from the ball when playing football. However, when Mr Proud made him litter monitor he showed an extraordinary talent for picking up litter. Years later he returned to visit the school and he was a millionaire, having made a fortune collecting scrap metal. So, if Mr Proud had not sent him out that first day into the playground with a dustpan and brush to retrieve all the discarded crisps and marbles, his talent would never have been realised!

I was still waiting to discover my special talent as it certainly wasn't attracting boys. Matthew Connelly barely made eye contact. I pinned all my hopes on my new supersize dice rubber breaking the ice because otherwise I would never get a look-in with Caroline and Lisa's enthusiastic prancing around him.

The pair of them reckoned they had grown real boobs and made sure that the boys overheard them mentioning it. Not only that but they apparently wore bras. Colleen Fahey, knew everything there was to know about puberty (gleaned from her three teenage brothers) and, said that they were just bikini tops and girls of eight can't grow boobs. I hoped this was true because it drove me mad the way Caroline and Lisa fed off male attention like they had been let loose in a sweet shop.

After morning assembly we went to our classrooms. We were in Junior Two which was located in the original part of the building, just across from the tin can assembly hall. Our desks were part of the original school furniture, complete with battered empty inkwells which were useful for sharpening pencils into if you didn't have any friends to meet at the bin for a pencil sharpening session. The desks were engraved with decades of student signatures and once a term Mr Proud would send the prefects round with tins of beeswax and paper towels for us to polish them to save money on paying cleaners. It didn't work; it just layered beeswax into the signatures which we would gouge out with a compass during mental arithmetic when we didn't know the answers and wanted to pretend we were invisible.

Mr Proud certainly saved a fortune on hiring manual labour by using his pupils for various jobs. Rather than complaining to our parents about it and our parents then issuing social media threats, these tasks were a source of delight and status. Litter duty I believe is now used as a punishment for badly behaved children. Back then it was a status symbol to walk around the playgrounds with a metal bin, retrieving crisp packets from drains with your bare hands while dreaming of turning it into a multi-million-pound business. Some of the boys would be specially chosen each year to repaint the rocks that held the tin can assembly hall and the temporary classrooms up white so they looked nice and clean. Even the most intellectually challenged pupil could be found a worthwhile job to do. Once Mr Proud made Clyde Clancy, who used to take bites out of floats during swimming lessons, the Christmas Tree Monitor. His job was to guard the school Christmas tree each breaktime (presumably in case it sprouted legs and did a runner) and he would sit next to it with a self-satisfied, if slightly glazed, expression, until the bell rang.

I feel I really should mention something here about inclusion in schools in the 80s for children with additional needs. Although there were a few schools in existence for children with severe or sensory disabilities, all children, regardless of ability, were pooled together in the same classrooms. We had few labels then, no statements of special educational needs for these children. Although we had fortunately moved on from the days of the dunce's cap and singling out slower learners for corporal punishment we had not yet started to label children with the kaleidoscope of conditions they get diagnosed with now. These children grew up believing (at least in their formative years) that they were just normal kids. No child was a 'problem', no child was set impossible goals. They were just taught to do their best and if their best wasn't quite as academic as their classmate then they just had to find their 'gift,' like the scrap metal collector I have already mentioned, and Mr Proud would try to help them discover it.

There was one boy who used to come to our school sometimes who was an extreme example. Michael Murphy had very few communication skills. At breaktime he would run up and down the length of the playground flapping his hands and shouting 'Wahoo! Wahoo!' which earned him the nickname, 'Wahoo Boy' (please remember we were only about eight years old at the time and not versed in political correctness). He couldn't write, he couldn't collect the litter and the teachers must have despaired for a while. Mr Proud watched him with a tortured expression from his study overlooking the playground each breaktime for weeks. He eventually noticed something about Michael. Michael was a stickler for routine and order. Mr Proud decided to stop ringing the brand new electric school bell and instead at the beginning and end of every breaktime gave Michael the old metal handheld school bell. He told him that it was his job to go round the classrooms at the start of break and at hometime and ring the bell to let the children know it was time to leave class. In a short time the sight of Michael approaching with his bell ringing and 'Wahooing' was something for everyone to get excited about. He was still known as 'Wahoo Boy' but he became like a pseudo member of staff and although he couldn't say much he revelled in his important job and his status. He only stayed at our school for a year before he was moved to a specialist school but in the time he was there I'd like to think he was happy and he felt valued.

Miss McCoughney our teacher reminded me of Lady Diana. In her early twenties, she was quite new to teaching and full of enthusiasm but could be quite nervous at times and had a habit of dropping her gaze and looking up at people through blue mascara. She wasn't married yet but she really wanted to be. She just couldn't find the right sort of boyfriend. We were her first class after her teacher training college and she adored us; in return we drove her half crazy. I will never forget the time we went for our weekly swimming lesson at Stirchley Baths and she forgot to do a headcount. When we returned to school we realised that Paul Walton and Clyde Clancy had been left behind. How we laughed! Poor Miss McCoughney! She was crying and visibly out of her mind with panic. She ran to get Mr Proud to help and I don't know if she was more scared of the reprimand she would get from him or the harm that might befall the two boys.

Mr Proud rushed to his car and drove straight to the swimming baths to make enquiries. They were not there. No one had seen them. He then followed the route back to the school, stopping to check out nearby parks, still no sign of them. He returned to school worried and agitated to tell Miss McCoughney that he needed to call the police. The whole class eavesdropped enthusiastically while whispering exciting conspiracy theories. Maybe they had been abducted by aliens! While this very tense exchange was taking place between Mr Proud and Miss McCoughney the two boys strolled casually in, coats tied around their necks like capes. Turns out they had spotted a dream opportunity by hanging out at the swimming pool lockers and retrieving the ten-pence pieces left by visitors that had not quite worked out the coin return mechanism. They had gathered their ten-pence pieces with glee and then walked the three miles back to school stopping at every sweet shop on the way, snapping up ten-pence-mixes to their hearts' content. They were now throwing their spoils on the desks and we were diving on them like a pack of starving hyenas. It took a roar from Mr Proud to make us all jump and shrink away back to our respective desks. Clyde Clancy and Mark Walton were then marched off to Mr Proud's office to sit in silence until home time. One thing was certain, Clyde Clancy and Mark Walton had discovered their special gift; they may have been limited in academic skills and had to sit on the 'thickie' table in our classroom but they had the gift of entrepreneurship.

Miss McCoughney loved us so much that once, as a special treat, we were invited to a play afternoon at her house where she lived with her parents and sisters. I'm talking the whole class here, and our parents were only too delighted to let us go for a few hours. We had a great time playing in the garden and we were even bought a Wimpy lunch by Miss McCoughney's dad. I suppose the suspicious minds of today would see this as potential grooming. It wasn't, it was just a fabulous day out.

Birthday Parties

Wimpy, the predecessor of McDonald's, was the culinary Holy Grail. To have a Wimpy meal was a special experience in itself, probably because it was a welcome change from the bland microwaved offerings and Findus Crispy Pancakes we got fed at home. The Wimpy meal, for an 80s child, was the equivalent of the Michelin-starred restaurant for an adult today, and a Wimpy birthday party, the equivalent of a day on a celebrity yacht.

Tony and I were some of the first kids in our class to have a Wimpy party. I remember it well. The entertainment consisted of meeting the famous Mr Wimpy himself. A six-foot foam mascot dressed as a Beefeater, with no eyes, just an enormous nose which was his only facial feature. He wasn't cute, he wasn't cuddly, he couldn't speak or wave, and he used to silently chase the birthday child and their guests – presumably to make the event more entertaining. Some marketing brainbox had actually come up with the idea that a Beefeater mascot, traditionally used to guard prisoners in the Tower of London, was appropriate. To make him even more 'appealing' he was made in the image of a chode: the mythical penis that is wider than it is tall. Today, this kind of mascot is the stuff of horror films but in the 80s it was a special treat that parents would even be willing to pay for. I think maybe this is why people from our generation are no wimps. You have never really known your adrenaline kick in until you've been chased by a six-foot chode masquerading as a prison guard. It was like an initiation ceremony for the trials of adulthood. Wimpy restaurants were eventually phased out by the emergence of McDonald's in Britain in the 80s... and their mascot was a terrifying clown!

The Wimpy party Tony and I had was a diversion from the traditional birthday party at home that children always used to have before the 80s. It paved the way for birthday parties to come. Before this time, for children, birthday parties were just as exciting as they are now but they didn't mean eye-watering financial outlay for parents and a tonne of stress and pressure to put on a show that was not only unique but at least as good as their kids' friends. As a parent now myself I have been to parties where the stress and effort involved is etched all over the faces of the birthday child's parents as they screech and sweat over the entertainers potentially not turning up, the themed decor not flowing properly, and getting the right angle of the three-tier cake for their Instagram feed. I went to one party last year where the child's entire family dressed as superheroes, which was fine for the parents, but I suspect that the 'geriatric man' sitting in a corner with glasses over his morph suit, looking like he'd pissed himself, might have been doing so under duress.

There was nothing wrong with birthday parties before fast food restaurants started to do them. You would turn up at someone's house, run around screaming and bursting balloons for a while, before settling down to a mighty meal of iced gems, fairy cakes, sausage rolls and fizzy pop. It was topped

53

off by the pièce de résistance: the birthday cake, always home made and often in the form of a hedgehog with Cadbury's buttons for spikes or a Swiss roll dog. After this there were the traditional games of musical bumps, musical statues and pass the parcel, played with much healthy competition. Then you would go home, leaving the house like a war zone, and the birthday child's mother would clean up. Sometime later in the 80s the Wimpy and McDonald's parties became popular. For the mothers they saved a lot of cleaning time and food preparation, for the children there was the delight of the burger and fries meals that we never ever got to eat at home. There usually weren't any traditional games on offer – the entire entertainment consisted of meeting the mascot.

Mr Wimpy made his hotly anticipated debut at mine and Tony's birthday party as a horde of seven-year-olds screamed in excitement and circled him. As he began to chase us some bright spark decided to ask if he was a boy or a girl (it was probably one of the 'thickies' as the clue was in the name 'Mr Wimpy') and when he didn't answer, as he had no mouth or power of speech, this child decided to get on the floor and look under his outfit for evidence. We all copied as we were curious to know what was underneath Mr Wimpy's costume. All I remember was that he got a bit irate at several kids poking and prodding him in his nether regions and he started to do a kind of wee-wee jog. It was no use as by this point some of the party guests were stamping on his enormous foam shoes to get him to keep still. Then a miracle occurred as we found he could suddenly speak, even if it was a very bad word. He tried to run away but as his shoes were pinned to the floor he just fell over and started rolling around, unable to get up due to the weight and roundness of his costume. It was like being imprisoned in one of those sumo suits. We thought it was tremendous fun so we started to pile on top of him as he shouted loudly for help. It was a shame when the game finished and all the staff had to leave the counter and drag him away. One of the managers sheepishly brought out our presents from Mr Wimpy, apologising that he would be unable to give them to us in person. We were given a joke kit (joke shops were a thing back then) complete with whoopee cushions, itching powder and disappearing ink, which we would employ on the various staff when we returned to school there was nothing like a prank for entertainment.

Practical Jokes

Pranking the teachers was one of the most celebrated activities of our school days. I very much doubt that this would be tolerated now, we would probably be labelled as having emotional and behavioural difficulties and referred to social services. In the 80s, as long as nobody was hurt or bullied then practical jokes were just practical jokes and there was no need to call a government Cobra meeting over them. We never pranked Mr Proud of course, due to respect and fear of the consequences. However, there were a few of the newly qualified teachers, like Miss McCoughney, whom we loved to prank before they gained their confidence, but it was never malicious and we had a good chuckle with them afterwards and they would always get us back. Miss McCoughney pretended that a compulsory Cadbury's purple and white uniform was coming to St Anthony's, which caused much panic in the playground when we really thought we would be walking around dressed like Dairy Milk bars for the rest of our school lives.

The other categories of staff that quite frankly deserved to be pranked were dinner ladies and school helpers who really should not have been let loose to work in a school at all because they hated children. There is an actual word for these types, 'misopedists,' and the Roald Dahl books that we read were full of tales of the delightful sticky ends that they would come to. We didn't have that type of luck at St Anthony's so the next best thing to lighten the misery of them being in charge was to prank them and not get caught. One school helper whom no one could stand was a retired music teacher called Miss Greatorex. We were used to retired teachers visiting the school to reminisce and take tea with Mr Proud and they were received with the greatest of enthusiasm as they would always bring giant boxes of Quality Street or Roses or read us a story in the afternoons. However, Miss Greatorex hung around the school like a lingering and anonymous presence that had to be dealt with. I think Mr Proud, in his typical manner, found her a task to do rather than making her feel unwanted. She became our occasional music teacher when our usual fun one, who sang about bananas in pyjamas and made us all laugh, was off on maternity leave or spending time with her babies, much to our disappointment.

Miss Greatorex was tall, bony and fierce, hair scraped back into a bun and always topped with a yellow fur hat with black flecks that looked like a fruit cake. She also had these thick bottle-top glasses with extra flip-up screens. When she shouted at you, which was often, and usually for some minor misdemeanour like singing a note out of tune, these top lenses used to flip up like she was about to shoot red Dalek beams. You would be half expecting her to shout, 'Exterminate!' as she would screech about how useless you were, with spittle flying out of her mouth the angrier she became.

She only had time for her 'sight readers' who were a few blatant favourites who played the recorder the best. She used to get them to congregate with her around the piano. 'Where are my sight readers?' she would shriek when she had had enough of the fact that our class sounded like a zombie chorus, and those damn lenses would flip up and she would scan the room. Along would skip the favourites, Caroline Harper and Lisa Edmunds, with their smug faces and immaculate hair, and they would spend the rest of the lesson in a little world of their own belting out a hymn with Miss Greatorex singing loudest and spitting furthest of them all. The rest of us would be condemned to stare at the notes on the page in silence until the bell went. One time, Colleen, in protest at the spitting tyrant, dared us all to bring our umbrellas and when we were banished to silence we just sat there with our umbrellas up giggling. The irony was lost on her, which was even funnier. She just called us all 'thick' for having our umbrellas up on such a lovely day and went back to her hymn.

The second possible candidate for pranking was one of the dinner ladies, Mrs Venn. Dinner ladies could be generalised as falling into two distinct personality types: maternal and squashy, who would let you hold their hand and walk around the playground with them when you missed your mom, or screeching harridans that were forever pulling you out of line and making you face the wall or stand on your chair. Mrs Venn was one of the latter. She was the queen of harridans, forever on a power trip because she was left in charge of us all while our teachers were contained in the staffroom, none the wiser. All I remember of this horrible woman was the way she used to march up and down the hall with her hands on her hips blowing a whistle while we ate. She would blow a whistle if you talked too loud, coughed, accidentally knocked over a cup, or any other reason she could find to make you stand on your chair while she screamed at you. I can't remember where any of the other dinner ladies were, probably cowering in the kitchen behind vats of pink blancmange. She would have been better off working as a prison guard.

We hotly debated our plan of action for some time but the actual execution of it was pure chance and we managed to prank both Miss Greatorex and Mrs Venn on the same day when the 'nit nurse' had been in to school. The nit nurse was a dreaded but necessary visitor for whom you would line up as she checked the roots of your hair for bugs. I seem to remember nits being less common in schools in the 80s then they are now. Apparently the nit nurse is now seen as an invasion of human rights or something like that. All the schools do now is send all parents a letter if one child has nits; the owner of the bugs remains anonymous. There is a tendency for some parents to say, 'Oh not my little darlings, we wash their hair every week,' without realising that head lice are like *Love Island* candidates – they rock up anywhere for free sex and a bit of exposure. They're not fussy.

Anyway, that morning we were in our recorder class, which in the absence of spare classrooms, always took place in the staff room. Miss Greatorex had been getting well into the swing of things and was getting us to play 'Greensleeves.' I use the word 'play' in the loosest sense, because anyone who has ever been subjected to the recorder being 'played' will know that even a good rendition is the equivalent of a metal claw being slowly dragged down a blackboard. When Mrs Greatorex got into her recorder playing her saliva would trickle out of the bottom of the instrument, but did she show a hint of embarrassment? Not at all! She would keep going until the string of saliva was hanging over her knees before pausing to bark at the nearest child, 'Get me a paper towel!' without so much as a 'please'. She would then flick the saliva trail away, not caring if it hit anyone, and then keep playing.

On this day we were talking non-stop about the nit nurse, speculating on who may have fallen victim to the six-legged beasts this time round. Due to the nature of the conversation we were all scratching our heads something terrible, imagining a nit party going on up there. The conversation eventually affected Miss Greatorex, who had to stop playing, take off her giant fruit cake hat, put it on the table and start scratching her head furiously too. She was not at all happy with us and bellowed loudly at our insolence and lack of attention before storming off to complain to Mr Proud. It was by chance that she left that monstrosity of a hat upon the table.

She didn't come back before the bell went so we decided to put the hat on a plate on a tea tray and surround it with a nice selection of biscuits that the teachers liked to treat themselves to with their cuppa at breaktime. We then put the entire display away in the cupboard and rapidly left the room, wishing we could see the looks on our teachers' faces when they received a lovely cake to go with their biscuits that day.

We were on a high when we went into to the tin can that day, in single file for lunch. I had had the Mr Wimpy whoopee cushion gift in school for a while and the whole class was desperate to have a go.

In our dinner hall the tables were set out in four long rows. Two were for those who were 'dinners' who we considered the unlucky, as they had to eat unappetising rubbish off pale green plates. School dinners have come a long way since those days. I think it is one of the only things that has actually improved with time (thanks to campaigns by a certain celebrity chef). I have yet to find any of my generation who actually misses primary school dinners. I think all of us started off our school lives with dinners and, unless you had been born without taste buds, you then had to wear your parents down with protest until they let you have sandwiches.

A typical school dinner consisted of two ice-cream scoops of Smash (powdered, processed potato) a portion of boiled cabbage and something that was labelled meat that looked rather like cat food, all disguised with a ladleful of lumpy gravy that didn't smell quite right. This was washed down with either tap water or on a 'good' day, pink milk in metal jugs poured into plastic beakers so scratched and cloudy, they could have been old toothbrush mugs fished out of bins. You were shouted at if you didn't eat most of it and had to go without pudding. Pudding wasn't much better It was either pink blancmange, which looked like the gunge Saturday morning game show hosts would dump on contestants' heads, or maybe a piece of fruit in a bowl. The delights of chocolate concrete in unlimited amounts as long as you had cash to pay for it were limited to secondary schools. I'll come to that later. For now your parents paid the school for your dinners and you got what you had the misfortune of being given.

The 'sandwiches' gang on the other tables were luckier. They didn't have anyone shouting at them if they chose not to eat. They had thermos flasks with Snoopy or Garfield pictures on, lovingly filled at home with squash, complete with E numbers to give them an extra perk during the afternoon. They had white bread sandwiches with the popular fillings of the time; I remember fish paste being a common one, along with Dairylea cheese spread, left-over meat from the Sunday roast, or tinned salmon with a sprinkling of vinegar. There would always be a packet of crisps: Piglets were bacon flavour crisps that were actually 3D shaped pigs, 'Fish 'n' Chips' were salt and vinegar and shaped like their name, then there were Skydivers and Football Crazy ball-shaped crisps. This would be polished off with a nice chocolate lunch bar with names like 54321 or United.

Fruit and wholemeal bread was the exception, unless you were my friend Ruth whose parents read things like *The Vitamin Bible* and *Tofu at Center Stage* because they believed that the E in E numbers stood for 'evil'. This was quite possibly because most of our mothers would be around to provide a home-cooked meal for us later that afternoon. 'Five a day' was an expression nobody ever used and I don't remember seeing any really fat kids at primary school. We burned off all our energy playing outdoors with E numbers to spur us on, so basically we enjoyed our packed lunches without interference. If we had a packet of crisps at breaktime and another to wash down our lunch with then that was nobody's business. Besides, it was an improvement on the pre-welfare-state diets of the working classes, which consisted of bread and dripping at regular intervals, so as far as anyone was concerned we were a thriving and well-fed nation.

The dinner ladies, as explained earlier, were generally inoffensive, maternal types. Mrs Venn was the exception as she patrolled up and down those lines of tables blowing her stupid whistle and looking for children to punish. She would often make us eat our dinners in silence so it was a source of great delight when the silence was broken by one brave member of our class letting the whoopee cushion do its best job. The entire hall collapsed into hysterical laughter. Mrs Venn charged up the aisle like a rhino.

'Who did that?' she roared, trembling with adrenaline and

rage. There were no volunteers so she picked out a couple of kids who were smiling a bit too much and made them stand on their chairs. We passed the whoopee cushion along and kept the hilarious noises going, with more and more children chosen to stand on their chairs as an example. Eventually, the offending item was discovered and thrown in the bin, but that was not the end of it.

There were always a few boys who could be relied upon to make super-loud farting noises from their armpits while pumping one arm up and down like a lame bird trying to take off. I don't know how they did it but I just remember that if it was perfectly timed it was hilarious. So, in every forced silence during that dinnertime a random farting noise would come from somewhere in that room. Eventually there were so many children standing on chairs that when Mr Proud came in to investigate the noise he looked at half the school standing on chairs and asked Mrs Venn if we happened to have an infestation of mice. She was sacked shortly after that. She's probably terrorising nursing home staff today.

Family Holidays Before They Were 'Foreign'

The only family that I knew of who usually went abroad for their summer holidays in the early 1980s were the Paynes. They went to gîtes in Brittany. Their days were spent wandering around markets; they ate cheese and drank wine like there was no tomorrow, and probably stayed up late in a warm garden debating literature, culture and politics without a fellow Brit or a tabloid newspaper in sight. My mother found the whole concept very odd. She had been lucky enough to travel abroad with my father when they were courting and had seen Tunisia and Spain, but abroad was not the place to take children she would say with disapproval, as if the mysterious 'abroad' was made up entirely of war zones. Many of her contemporary baby boomer friends had never ventured outside of England and had no desire to. There were horror stories that came from people who had been, such as, that there was never anywhere to get a decent cup of tea, none of the ignorant 'abroad' people spoke 'the language,' and the combination of funny food, dangerous tap water and extreme temperatures made your skin go the colour of ketchup and, to add insult to injury, you ended up sitting on the toilet for days. Abroad was an experience not for the faint-hearted, and of course never for a family holiday!

Our holidays were very similar to those enjoyed by our own parents when they were small. We would travel by car to some seaside town and stay in a B&B or a caravan or sometimes a Butlin's chalet. The weather, as always in England, would be unpredictable. If it was good then there would be sandy beaches and dunes to explore and rock pools full of small crabs, and if you were lucky, a starfish or some small fish that you could catch in your hand-held nets. There would be shells and fossils to collect in your plastic buckets and you could eat picnics on the beach, fish and chips for tea and endless amounts of soft ice cream in cones. If it rained it was trickier but you could trawl the endless gift shops looking for rock to take back to your friends at school and maybe some small novelty ornaments like shells with eyes stuck on (yes I know they sound ridiculous, and they were, but children have always found wondrous qualities in things that adults would put in a bin). Sometimes it rained a lot and you were stuck indoors playing cards, listening to the rain pounding on the roof. It was occasionally boring but for the most part we had vivid imaginations and didn't rely on expensive day trips and screen time to keep us occupied.

Expectations for holidays were a lot lower back then. The whole point of the holiday was to take a break from the usual daily routine, of work, housework, and school to spend some family time together. We didn't demand that our accommodation or the services provided to us were aspirational. If we book a holiday today we fully expect our surroundings to be more luxurious than our own homes; we expect to be waited on hand and foot for our meals, and we expect housekeeping services. If we don't get them or they fall even slightly below what we would expect the most privileged members of society to have then we go complaining loudly to anyone who will listen, and demand our money back. Unfortunately, we have become 'brattish' and self-centred, which is a very sad observation. As for family time, forget it. If there is a kids' club or crèche then the children must be dispatched there immediately so the adults can have time to themselves. If there is no Wi-Fi in the restaurants or hotel then this is unacceptable, as we may be forced to actually speak to one another!

I remember that most of our holiday accommodation was below the standard that we would have at home. If we stayed in a caravan, the two-ringed calor gas hob meant that meals were more basic. There were more sandwiches and salads as there was nowhere to cook the Findus Crispy Pancakes, no deep-fat fryer for the homemade chips (oven chips were yet to be invented) and no microwave. In fact, there were no flashy gadgets at all. Far from being a problem it was a bonus, especially for our mothers who had a week or two away from cooking and baking. The 'bathroom' in a caravan consisted of a cubicle with just a toilet. It was so small that your knees would touch the door. If you were in a B&B then an en-suite bathroom was a rarity. It was perfectly acceptable to be sharing with other guests. It was easier for us kids not to have a nightly bath. One more chore that our mothers got out of.

During the day, if we were on the beach or on a campsite, our parents generally sat around drinking tea (well, actually, if we were on a campsite many parents tended to disappear indoors for large parts of the day and left us to our own devices. I really don't want to know why but I like to think they were playing cards and eating rock rather than muddy my nostalgia). This left hordes of school-age kids wandering round and making their own gangs. It was always great fun to go and find other kids who 'talked funny' and have a good laugh at their accents. We did not believe that we could possibly have an accent of our own! We would then proceed to grill each other about life up north or down south as if they were aliens from other planets. We often became firm friends and exchanged addresses at the end of the holiday so that we could write to each other as pen-friends, which we usually managed for a few weeks.

More 'Foreigners'

One day I went to Ruth's to try a tofu stir-fry and there in the kitchen, dressed in a silk kimono with what looked like knitting needles in her hair, and way too much talc on her face, was a real Japanese lady in traditional dress.

'Make sure my mom doesn't find out about this,' I whispered anxiously to Ruth. 'She'll only flipping want one of her own!'

She got one anyway.

The Paynes, through their positions at the university, played host family to foreign students on placements throughout the course of the year. Mostly they were French, Italians or Japanese. They would attend college in the daytime and then return to the home of their hosts, who would feed them an English dinner and chat around the table in order to improve their English speaking skills. The Paynes received a fee for their hospitality. My mom thought it was an amazing idea. Dad was sceptical at first about having a stranger living in the house but my mom persuaded him that being a host family would provide a useful second income for us and would pay for our summer holidays.

We did have a Japanese girl too at first, her name was Miki and she was lovely. I knew her arrival was going to be a bit controversial when my dad went to pick her up from the coach station and my mom pulled Grandad Jimmy into the utility room for a quiet word.

'If I hear you say anything about Pearl Harbour there will be serious trouble, do you understand?'

Grandad Jimmy emerged looking sheepish.

Miki introduced us to a kind of dried seaweed snack that looked like paper and stunk like fish. She also introduced us to a type of raw seafood called sushi, so Nanny Pearl immediately taught her how to bake a Victoria sponge and a steamed pudding so her and her family could enjoy a nice treat when she went home.

Every few months we would get a new student, or sometimes two, in the spare room. Once we had a pair of young French boys sent to us, Terry and Patrice. They stick out in my memory the most because they seemed to Tony and me to be a bit stupid. They would have definitely been on the 'thickie' table at St Anthony's. The reality was that they were a fair bit younger than the other students we had been sent and had very little grasp of the English language. They used to sit huddled together, terrified, on the sofa. Tony and I would entertain them by sliding down the stairs in sleeping bags and by taking it in turns to stand on the coffee table and pretend to shoot each other before falling off and dying in front of them but they didn't even crack a smile, they just huddled a little closer. One day they gave us a peace offering of a whole pack of something called Wrigley's Juicy Fruit, which we had never been allowed before. We devoured the lot. That night we were extremely sick and kept throwing up grey pebble things in the sink. Convinced they had tried to poison us, the next day we prepared a plate of Rich Tea biscuits, took them in the lounge and before they ate them we drew a picture on each one in crayon, telling them it was an English tradition. We got on just fine after that.

Before they left they presented my mother with a beautiful box of shortbread that Nanny Pearl had helped them make. It was a lovely gesture, but she was rather baffled as to why they had crayoned 'Thank you Mrs Jones' on the back of each one along with a smiley face.

The first time we had an Italian come to stay with us my father was delighted, as he worked as a salesman for a menswear company called Ciro Citterio. He spent a long time telling her proudly all about the leading Italian brand and its fine suits and shirts. He had been selling 'Italian' clothing for a decade and was becoming increasingly frustrated when this teenage girl had never heard of them. 'Ciro Citterio!' he reminded her for the umpteenth time over the signature bolognese welcome dinner, rustled up especially for her arrival.

Ciara Colombo, from Milan, shrugged her shoulders and pushed her traditional Italian cuisine suspiciously around her plate

She shook her head. 'No, no Ciro Citterio.'

'You-know,' emphasised my father, dramatically slowing his speech down in order to spark a glimmer of familiarity. 'Famous-see-ro-sit-sit-ah-rio'. He gesticulated with wild hand movements at a pile of shirts in his ironing pile in the corner of the kitchen.

'No,' said Ciara again, listlessly stirring the spag bol around the plate.

'Maybe she would like a steak and kidney pie?' offered Nanny Pearl.

Shortly afterwards my dad found out that the famed Ciro Citterio had no connections with Italy at all. The company was the creation of some Asian entrepreneurs from Birmingham. He had been selling for them for nearly ten years and unwittingly passing on the fraud in his sales pitch. After a mild moral panic as he worked on commission and was very good at selling, he decided to carry on with his usual pitch, which he did very successfully until he retired in 2002.

Another 'foreigner' came into our white suburban existence quite unexpectedly. Our parish priest, Father McGuiness, was due to retire and everyone expected his replacement to be cast from the same mould and dispatched to our parish without causing the slightest ripple of gossip. I used to imagine that the archbishop created new priests in the manner of the Gizmo character from the Gremlins film. Someone would spray him with holy water and these little clones would pop out of his back ready to be dispatched all over the country. How else could all the priests be so alike in looks and mannerisms? They were always Irish, and frequently, had accents so broad that it was hard to understand some of the things they said. They all had kindly red faces and hadn't a clue what Grange Hill or Castle Grayskull was. They had no idea of the life that existed beyond the sanctuary of their candles, effigies and parables.

Every time Father McGuiness used to visit our class we would bombard him with enthusiastic questions and stories about what we were doing, what we saw on TV the night before and what we were having for tea and he would just look embarrassed and smile because he hadn't the faintest clue what was going on. We got the impression he lived in the chancery, existing on a diet of communion bread and red wine, as no one ever saw him in the shops. He was only ever comfortable in the confines of his church, where he would recite the same script a few times a week in his flowing robes of bright green or purple satin like an actor immersed in a play where he was the only character. There was a sermon every week that none of us children understood (something about sheep or people with flames on their heads). It made us feel either very sleepy or very fidgety and there was much nudging in the back or taps on the shoulder from our teachers encouraging us to pay attention. For many years I misheard a lot of the prayers and sermons. The Hail Mary seemed to mention how the 'liver was evil' and I imagined all my friends gagging at the sight of liver and onions.

Father McGuiness retired as quietly as a whisper. He was presented with a bottle of whisky by the mothers after his last mass. He smiled at us all, muttered something about hoping that there were some future priests and nuns in our midst, and then he floated slowly back into the chancery where presumably he would melt in a pile of green damask and whisky fumes.

It caused quite a stir when Father Hu Nguyen, a Vietnamese boat refugee and former Buddhist, showed up and told us to call him Father Simon. Unlike his predecessors, whose adult lives were so sheltered and out of touch they judged any non-conformism with harshness and the need for penance, Father Simon had known hardship and devastation and had lived, against the odds, to tell the tale.

As a young man he had escaped the brutal communist regime of Vietnam and boarded a crowded boat, with other refugees. After three days the boat ran out of petrol, food and water and so the group drifted helplessly for seventeen days. When one of the women on the boat went into labour and gave birth to a baby boy, Father Simon began to pray for the baby's life in desperation, and promised that if the baby lived he would dedicate his life to God. A few hours later the group was rescued by a British ship and all the refugees survived. Father Simon became the first ordained Vietnamese priest in Britain. He was proud to tell us his story and show us the newspaper article.

He was one of the happiest and most non-judgmental people I have ever met. He told us that the word 'Catholic' meant 'universal' and accepting of everyone. This was quite a diversion from his forebears and their closed minds. Father Simon's joy to be alive was infectious as he immersed himself fully in community life, whether it was helping out at our school cake sale, taking Christmas hampers to old people's homes or sitting discussing life and enjoying a cup of tea in someone's kitchen while they did the ironing. Father Simon was the reason that the church began to fill up (well, that and the way he would play Christian pop music and gospel music and put disco lights around the nativity scene). Everyone was sad when he had to leave for another parish and was replaced by another gremlin.

Midnight Feast

Tony and I both loved Michael Jackson and spent a lot of time trying to re-create his famous moonwalk dance. We were not very good at it. Tony also tried to re-create the breakdancing and body-popping routines that were the craze at the time. It was mostly a boy thing. I couldn't get into the sweat bands and spinning around on the floor like a dying beetle or almost knocking your teeth out in an attempt to be a worm on fast forward. I much preferred the carefully choreographed moves of Five Star and the smouldering over-the-shoulder glances into my dressing table mirror like Madonna.

The first time we were allowed out without an adult was when Brian King, in full breakdancing get-up, came to our house for a sleepover. He was the one I couldn't stand due to him being big-headed and full of crap. Anyway, there were two places we were desperate to go to. First, into our local village of Cotteridge to each select a 45-inch single to buy with our pocket money, and second, to our local sweet shop to choose a ten-pence-mix and various other sugar-laden treats for a midnight feast, a midnight feast being compulsory for any sleepover.

We walked up to Woolworths, Tony in a hot pink and blue shell suit combo, Brian, swaggering in breakdancer uniform of ski wear and knitted hat, and me letting the side down in a jumper covered in kitten pictures, snow-washed jeans and a Benetton cap. We spent a long time trying to decide between Michael Jackson's 'Billie Jean' or Men at Work's 'Down Under' before settling on both.

When we left we were distracted by some older boys in shiny bright shell suits and sweatbands breakdancing on pieces of lino at the side of the road. We were awestruck. They were totally oblivious to the deadpan faces of pensioners and housewives walking past doing their Saturday grocery shop. They had their ghetto blaster going and they were flinging themselves around and contorting into all types of shapes as their wet-look perms flopped all over the place. Brian King knew everything about break-dancing as he was apparently due to be signed to a record label because a music producer from New York had heard about his moves via the playground grapevine. After a few minutes he was deep in conversation with the older boys with his stupid street slang; everything was 'wicked' or 'skill' or 'safe' and I wanted the ground to swallow me up. Somehow, despite the complete implausibility of his connections, as Brian was a fat white choirboy in his other life, he managed to persuade the boys to let him and Tony join them and have a go at copying their moves and maybe even putting together a few new ones of their own.

I was left standing there awkwardly. A few minutes ago the three of us had been selecting cheesy pop records and now I was left holding a carrier bag of records and expected to make myself, an embarrassing, non-shell-suited girl, disappear. After a short while of shuffling from foot to foot awkwardly and not knowing whether to try and blend in with the Saturday shoppers or even more awkwardly attempt to join in with the boys, which was surely a choice I would regret, I decided to walk casually away leaving them to their jerking about, spinning and strange poses.

What to do now? There was only one place I knew of other than home and that was the corner sweet shop by our school. Known to us as Taylor's, it had been there since the turn of the century. They were a still a common sight in the 80s and often within a stone's throw of schools, which was marvellous as it would often be a priority to head over there at least once a week and experience the thrill of buying a ten-pence-mix. In those days ten pence went a long way and you could easily buy ten individual sweets for that, more if you counted the half-penny sweets. I didn't know my way round my local area at all but I knew the way from Cotteridge village to the sweet shop by my school and then home again and that was all I needed to know.

I arrived at Taylor's sweet shop with my adrenaline pumping with excitement over the sugar shopping spree I was about to embark on. I decided it would be best to buy everything ready for the midnight feast as Tony and Brian were clearly going to be tied up with their shopping centre choreography for some time.

The shop, being a weekend, was deserted instead of rammed with children shoulder to shoulder, pushing and shoving, to lay their eyes upon the wonders of sweets on display. It was going to be a real luxury to actually be able to take my time choosing, because choosing between so many sweets really was difficult and the more indecision and umming and ahhing you inevitably did, the more you could sense the overexcitement and urgency of the children in the queue behind you and their telepathic messages to hurry up so they could have a turn.

The jolly round shopkeeper waddled from behind the beaded

curtain separating her corner shop from her living quarters. I could smell chip pans and cigarette smoke from somewhere beyond this, and hear *Grandstand* on the TV. I just knew there was a middle-aged man in front of it waiting with baited breath to hear the football results, a Littlewoods pools slip on his lap, pen poised and ready.

'What can I get for you, Miss?'

I eyed the trays of sweets behind the glass counter. 'Three ten-pence-mixes please! And then I have an extra pound note to buy some other things!'

The shopkeeper picked up the sweet scoop and a pile of paper bags. My mouth watered. It was going to be a long afternoon!

After a record level of umming and ahhing I emerged into the sunshine with a carrier bag laden with pieces of sugar heaven. The boys would be so pleased. I had milk teeth, white mice, cola bottles, foam bananas and prawns, packs of rainbow bubblegum balls, bags of chocolate limes and lemon sherbets, bottles of banana and strawberry flavoured milk and even a few Fry's Chocolate Creams with the five different flavour soft centres, perfect for the indecisive consumer like myself. I practically skipped along the pavement. Then my heart stopped, for there sitting on the wall outside Taylor's were two people I certainly didn't want to see right then, the two most popular and over-confident girls in my class: Caroline Harper who had recently started calling herself 'Caz,' and Lisa Edmunds otherwise known as 'Leese'. My heart skipped a beat, and not in a good way.

They sat, self-assuredly swinging their legs, feet clad in hideous but oh-so-fashionable jelly shoes, matching jelly bags on their laps, bikini tops stuffed with socks under their t-shirts, smoking pretend cigarettes to make them look as cool as possible. These were not the candy cigarettes like the ones I had tucked carefully in my bag but the cooler ones made by rolling up paper, stuffing talcum powder inside and bog roll in each end. They were blowing enthusiastically through their pretend fags and shouting at imaginary friends in cars that drove past.

'See ya later, Shaz!"

'Hi Tracy! Are we going clubbing tonight?'

In their game they were cool young women, clad in the ultimate in trendy clothes and living fast-paced lives filled with boys, pop music and fags. I don't think Margaret Thatcher would have approved. To me, at that moment, they represented everything that I would never be: brimming with confidence, perfect hair, straight teeth, knowledge of every chart lyric, every fashion must-have and the ability to sit through one of Mr Proud's mental arithmetic tests without dread in their hearts and brain cell paralysis. 'Oh, hi Melanie!' they shouted in over the top familiarity. They made no eye contact. They were looking directly at the carrier bag in my hands. 'What you got there?'

Now I was in trouble. I took a step awkwardly towards them, conscious of my cute rather than fashionable clothes, my unmanageable hair and the gap between my teeth. I would have lied but I was rubbish at it.

'Brian King is staying over at our house. I bought stuff for a midnight feast.'

'Oh wow, let's have a look!'

Now don't get me wrong, these girls posed no risk to me, only to my sweets. Secondly, I was very aware that they had no desire to hang out with me because they found me fun or interesting, only for what I could do for them. I'd fallen for their tricks before when I was suddenly invited to Lisa's house after Christmas and instructed to bring my new Mr Frosty present. There was also the time when I was invited to tea at Caz's house and grilled non-stop on all the answers to every Brownie badge test I had ever taken, so that she could be like me and have badges all the way up her arms. Right now my sweetie treasures were under siege.

I showed them the contents of the carrier bag and let them run their talcum powered hands through the haul like they were jewels.

'You are so so lucky! We wish we could come to your house for a sleepover. Can you ask your mom?'

'No, she will say it's too short notice. Well, nice to see you. I'd better go. I'm supposed to be home by now,' I replied and started to walk away. To my dismay they started tottering after me, doing an odd stampy walk to keep their jelly shoes, which were mostly made of air anyway, from falling off, swinging their handbags and blowing clouds of talc dust in their wake.

I decided to walk faster. Surely I could lose them if I walked quickly enough and crossed the road a few times. It didn't work though, the faster I walked the faster they clip-clopped happily behind me. I decided to take a detour through the park. I wasn't entirely sure of the long way home, but I had been here before on Sports' Days and picnics and once I had lost them I could surely just turn round and retrace my steps. I thought of Tony and Brian and hoped that they were still rehearsing on the lino in Cotteridge and had not got home before me to find that I had disappeared with the combined pocket money.

The park route proved to be one of the worst decisions I had ever made. Most of our school seemed to be there, along with most of the kids from other schools in the area. The sight of me almost galloping by this stage, with Caz and Leese somewhere in a plume of talc behind me, attracted too much attention. There were no dinner ladies around to help out now.

'She's having a midnight feast!' screamed Caz in excitement.

'She's been to Taylor's and she's bought most of the shop!'

Quickly kids began to drop off the caterpillar climbing frame, they shot off the roundabout and stuck their heads over the top of the sandpit, and before long I was like the Pied Piper. If there were parents anywhere around here the kids were too quick for them. The scene was starting to resemble one of my scary dreams but I had no option to leap as high as a house or fly away. I now knew how Jesus felt when he had to feed the five thousand when he had only five loaves and two fishes. I was racking my brain as I ran trying to think of how he managed to get out of that one.

In the end I flung five foam bananas and two shrimps at my disciples Caz and Leese and told them that if they divided them up, like in the story of Jesus and the five thousand, there was just a small chance they would feed half of Bournville's children. They looked at me suspiciously.

'What Bible story does Jesus have a banana in? I don't know that one.'

'Oh you must know the sermon of the Banana on the Mount, it comes after the Parable of the Prodigal Shrimp.'

'Don't be silly, we weren't born yesterday!'

'Well just try it first, remember, God works miracles if you believe in him.' I left them staring perplexed at the seven sweets in their hands as I ran away from people for the second time that day.

Thankfully I didn't encounter any more embarrassing situations on my way home and I arrived back with my sugar treasure to be greeted with a hero's welcome by Brian and Tony, even if they didn't let me crash in their room.

Miss McCoughney Gets a Boyfriend

By the summer of 1986 Miss McCoughney was still not married and it bothered her. Our class, especially the girls, was very close to Miss McCoughney and often used to volunteer to stay after home-time to help with wall displays or paint themes on the glass panes of her classroom. She was a really popular teacher and we all thought the world of her. Prince Andrew was soon to marry Sarah Ferguson and there was wedding fever in the tabloids. 'Fergie' was a popular figure and the girls at school, and young unmarried women like Miss McCoughney, had already started copying her style in the hope that they too might attract a prince. 'Fergie bows' were the ultimate hair accessory and we enthusiastically plonked the bright oversized bows on our heads. The sailor-style collar and huge puffed sleeves like balloon biceps was another Fergie fashion choice that was much admired and copied amongst young girls and women. Never mind attracting princes, when all these things were worn at the same time, they repelled all males within a five-mile radius.

'I can't believe I'm still single at my age!' lamented Miss McCoughney to the poster of Paul Young she kept on the wall next to the blackboard, lopsided Fergie bow sliding down her head in the effort to stay in place. It was breaktime and she was attempting to mark books at her desk as Yaw, Matthew Connelly and I stood on bookcases painting mermaids and knights on the high window panes.

'How old are you, Miss?' asked Matthew.

'I'm twenty-five,' she said sadly.

'That's not old, Miss,' he replied. 'Mr Gray is thirty-one and he's never been married.'

Mr Gray was another popular teacher. His drama classes and his impersonations of the other staff and famous people used to have us in stitches. We thought Mr Gray's real name was Frankie because once he wore a t-shirt under his suit that said 'Frankie says Relax' instead of a shirt because he was cool like that, but Mr Proud made him put his shirt and tie back on. Also some of the trendy girls used to follow him round singing, 'Frankie! Do you remember me?' and it always made him smile.

'Mr Gray won't ever get married,' said Miss McCoughney.

'Why not, Miss?'

'Never you mind,' laughed Miss McCoughney.

'He's a friend of Dorothy,' said Yaw, matter-of-factly. Miss McCoughney spat her coffee back into her mug.

I was totally lost by now but pretended to know what Yaw meant. I felt a bit embarrassed that I couldn't follow the conversation and I didn't know who Dorothy was so I thought it was best to pretend I knew.

'Oh I know her! Why can't you find a boyfriend?'

'I don't know, maybe I should go on a diet?'

'Maybe you should go to Weight Watchers, Miss, my mom does,' volunteered Matthew

'Matthew, you're not supposed to say that! You're supposed to say I don't need to go on a diet!'

'But you just said it,' said Matthew, baffled as he climbed down from the bookcase. 'You're just as bad as my mom. She asked me if she looks fat in her jeans. I told her she looked massive and she started shouting and sent me to my room. It's a sin to tell lies but when I tell the truth I get in trouble. Man! I will never understand women!,'

'My dad says men like curvy women, Miss, they like something to grab on to. He says his worst nightmare is waking up to that Mad Lizzie off TV-AM, all teeth and no knockers!' said Yaw.

'Right children, I think it's nearly time for the bell. Why don't you boys go and find Michael Murphy and let him know.'

Matthew and Yaw put down their paintbrushes and looked at each other in surprise. 'But break just started!'

'Well, it could take you a while to find Michael so off you go!'When they had gone she smiled at me and shook her head as if to say, 'What are they like?'

but I knew she was sad. She wanted a boyfriend and maybe I should help her find one. So, as I was no Cilla Black, I did the next best thing and prayed to God every night for weeks.

By Christmas that year, after much praying, secret playground crisis meetings and general agonising that our beloved Miss McCoughney was destined to grow into a cranky old maid like Miss Greatorex, my friends and I decided that this was a battle that was destined to be lost. As far as we could gather Miss McCoughney loved discos and and meeting people but she was far too busy at weekends with her lesson planning and (judging by the contents of her desk drawer) making mix tapes of Paul Young and similar mullet-headed crooners.

Anyway, the novelty had worn off and we had something

else to get excited about: the latest school trip. We were off to Aston Hall for a Christmas celebration. That year we had been to Aston Hall twice already. Once for the bog standard look around the Jacobean Manor House with our clipboards and worksheets, the second time for a traditional autumn day of wassailing, which involved invoking an old English tradition of singing around apple trees, putting toast in the branches and then much roaring and bashing of pots and pans to ward off evil spirits, much to our delight. The third and upcoming visit promised to be the most exciting; we were all going to dress in period costume and sing carols by candlelight. It was going to be so much fun!

It certainly had been the longest school project we had ever known! It had lasted almost a year now. In between visits the Aston Hall tour guide, an immensely likeable, mullet-headed, moustached man called Mr Roberts, would come and visit our class and tell us ghost stories and legends from times gone by. We really thought that we must be the most interesting class that had ever graced Aston Hall and that they had been keen to keep our acquaintance by inviting us time and time again.

The great day came and everyone had badgered their parents to put together the most authentic Jacobean costume they could muster. With the absence of the internet and ready-made fancy dress back then, the class efforts varied depending on the enthusiasm and school involvement of our parents. Pam Sullivan, who was one of the most active members of the PTA and who ran the school cookery club, led the procession from our school down to Kings Norton station. What a motley crew we were, drifting along the pavement in homemade mob caps and full-length gowns, with Pam leading the way. Others had concertina paper ruffs around their necks, while one child,

85

who shall remain nameless because their parents were dumb as a box of frogs and had missed the point of the exercise completely, was clad in one large square of cardboard on his front and another on his back with crêpe paper 'cheese' bits flapping about and the words 'Jacobs' written across him.

I was loving wearing one of Nanny Pearl's old skirts which was just the right length on me to sweep the floor, and the blouse I'd constructed myself out of a net curtain. I felt like Helena Bonham-Carter in *A Room with a View,* wrong century I know but I could pretend, couldn't I? I was also excited to have been chosen to sing a solo rendition of 'The Twelve Days of Christmas' at the hall and if I had been singing on *Top of the Pops* it would have been just as epic a moment in my ten years on Earth.

We got some strange looks on the way to the train station but it was nothing compared to what we received when we walked from Aston train station to the Hall, through the run-down industrial backstreets. Aston was a melting pot of working-class multi-cultures and coming from an almost exclusively white suburb it felt surreal. No neatly manicured front lawns here but row upon row of ugly old terraces with grey, crumbling front walls. All around us were strange cooking smells, languages we did not recognise, women who were dressed like the Virgin Mary and men in pyjamas with Tommy Cooper hats. They stopped with their shopping and their doorstep chatting to stare at the bizarre procession of white children dressed like ghosts of the past (and savoury snacks). It was such a relief to reach the open space and calm of the Aston Hall grounds.

Mr Roberts greeted us at the front door of the Great Hall looking like something out of the cartoon 'Dogtanian and the

Three Muskehounds.' He was the perfect cavalier with his velvet breeches and flamboyant feathered cap. He ushered us into the enormous house, which was all dark wood and magical candlelight, kissing Miss McCoughney's hand, making her flush red as a tomato. The sound of harps and flutes danced across the mahogany floors and we were in awe of a great table laden with a pig's head and stuffed peacock in the centre and spilling over with more recognisable party food.

After we had stuffed our faces and played party games it was time for my solo and, despite being so nervous that my voice started off sounding like a lamb being electrocuted, I managed to pull off the 'Twelve Days of Christmas' so well that all the mom helpers and some of the girls started crying with emotion. I thought that it was down to my unique vocal talent but when I came down from my famous singer fantasy I saw that Mr Roberts was down on one knee in front of the Christmas tree and Miss McCoughney was saying yes.

I thanked the Father, the Son, the Holy Spirit, Mary, Joseph and all the saints, that my prayers had been answered and Miss McCoughney was finally going to be a bride and not a spitting, screeching, mad old woman with a fruitcake for a hat.

Weddings and Celebrations

Miss McCoughney's wedding was in the summer of 1987 and naturally we were all going. I don't remember if we were officially invited but we badgered her so much that before long we knew where the church and reception were taking place.

By now I was eleven and getting more girly which meant the Star Wars figures had been consigned to a drawer somewhere. My games often consisted of planning my wedding and I was envious when my classmates were chosen to be a bridesmaid for some relative during the school holidays. I was never going to get the chance to be a bridesmaid. I didn't even have any unmarried aunts or sisters to rely on. I was never going to wear a pastel Bo-Peep-style dress.

The boys at school didn't seem to share the same enthusiasm. They avoided wedding talk at all cost. If they were unlucky they were made to be a pageboy during the school holidays and they went to great lengths to make sure that no one would find out. Having pageboys amongst your wedding attendants was a bit of a craze in the 80s. They were like the ultimate wedding fashion accessory for brides wanting to emulate Diana and Fergie. Girls wanting to be bridesmaids were ten-a-penny, boys who wanted to be pageboys were as rare as Boy George's girlfriends and so any cute-looking small boy, irrespective of whether he was related to the bride and groom or not, would be plucked from wherever and made to don white tights, patent shoes with buckles and a sailor suit, or if they were especially unfortunate, something velvet with a feathered cap. Tony still breaks out in a cold sweat at the memory of the one time this happened to him. Fortunately, Miss McCoughney had found two small boys playing in her neighbour's garden to be her pageboys, which meant that all the boys in our class could crawl out from under their desks and breathe a sigh of relief.

The girls, and there were about fifteen of us in our class, were quite convinced she was going to choose some of us as bridesmaids. Caz and Leese reckoned they were best suited for the job and breaktimes were suddenly taken over by them having to practise their walking up and down the length of the playground while the rest of us were persuaded to play photographers. Leese even brought in her Communion photos to remind Miss McCoughney of how glorious she had looked in a full-length satin dress complete with tiara, veil, high heels, handbag, satin gloves, diamanté-studded bible on a chain topped off with a huge parasol. She had been allowed to wear this over-the-top get up because she had screamed the bridal shop down, refused to attend her communion and then gone on hunger strike until her parents gave in. She then spent the day swinging all her accessories around and photobombing everyone else's photographs. If she could have attached a pumpkin coach to her arm on that day along with the rest of the shiny white paraphernalia then she would have.

For my First Holy Communion I just knew I had to have a huge white dress with balloon sleeves, sparkly beads and a veil. After all, wasn't it a trial run for my wedding day?

My mom and Nanny Pearl had other ideas. It was not a

wedding or a fashion show, it was a sacrament. So, despite being dragged round various bridal shops and despite my pleading, downturned mouth and wistful gazes at the elaborate displays, I was denied even the opportunity of trying on a single pastel merengue.

'If you have one of those outfits you will only be embarrassed in the future when you look at the photos,' said my mom as I longingly stroked a white parasol.

'Absolutely ridiculous,' said Nanny Pearl as she pursed her mouth disapprovingly at the sight of a seven-year-old girl emerging from the changing room like a ship's sail, while her mother dabbed her eyes with a handkerchief. 'I blame the mother,' she carried on within earshot, 'trying to turn the whole thing into the wedding she never had.' There was no point in me throwing a strop like Leese had done. If I had gone on hunger strike Nanny Pearl would have then given everyone extra portions of pudding and cake, and made sure they ate them in front of me while giving a running commentary on what I was missing out on. As for me, threatening to boycott my own big day, well they would have said that would have been up to me and at least I would have saved my dad a bit of money.

They settled on a 'sensible' knee-length lace dress with a cardigan and plain white head-dress for me. I was so disappointed. They were right though. Somewhere in Caz and Leese's family photographs are some very embarrassing shots of small girls swathed in so many layers of satin, nets and fake bling it looks like an explosion on a *Dynasty* set.

It was a small consolation that Leese didn't get her way with Miss McCoughney. She told us she couldn't possibly have chosen between all of her lovely girls so she had regretfully asked her two sisters to do the honours. Instead, she let all the girls accompany her wedding-dress shopping. We went on the train into town and it was as though the circus had arrived. Fifteen ten-year-old girls racing excitedly around bridal shops, touching everything and squealing with delight at the displays. At least every shop we went to we managed to get completely to ourselves.

All the talk of weddings and happily ever after made me focus even more on something that had been pre-occupying my thoughts for some time. I was falling in love with Matthew Connelly, a boy in my class who made me laugh and stared at me a little too much. I could no longer walk past a mirror or a car door without checking my hair and if he happened to be within earshot I suddenly forgot what I was having a conversation with my friends about and began to feel my face burning up. Falling in love was inconvenient and embarrassing when I was with my friends. When I was alone it was delightful and day dreamy, and when I was around him and he caught my eye and smiled, well, that made my heart beat faster and my grin bigger than any Star Wars merchandise ever had. It was a significant change that was taking place in me. What with the new self-consciousness and the willingness to wear a flouncy dress without a meltdown, I barely recognised myself but I didn't care.

Tony was changing too. A few years previously, Mom virtually had to frog-march him to have a bath but now he was going into the bathroom voluntarily like it was a magical trip to Narnia. He would emerge hours later smelling of Hai Karate, with his hair gelled and combed with such precision it resembled melted plastic, and he would pretend he had only been to use the loo. Unlike me he didn't get embarrassed. He had a photo of Linda Lusardi in his drawer that he had cut out of *The Sun* newspaper and when Ruth and I found it and drew some clothes on her he was very annoyed and had to go through the school craft cupboard for ages until he found another one.

The day of Miss McCoughney's wedding finally arrived and I dressed in a Freeman's catalogue outfit that I had nagged Mom to get me. I wore white and green stripy trousers with a cropped bright green jacket with shoulder pads and gold buttons, green Fergie bow in my hair and slip-on shoes. I teamed it with a touch of baby blue eyeliner and mascara and a frosty pink lipstick borrowed from mom's make-up bag. I gazed at myself in excitement in front of the mirror. I looked so grown up; Matthew Connelly just had to notice me in this. I just needed to add a few plastic green beads and matching hooped earrings and my seductive wedding guest look would be complete. Eat your heart out Madonna! Tony swaggered from his room, dripping in gel, sporting Farah trousers, slip-on shoes with tassels, a Sergio Tacchini jacket and towelling sweat bands round his wrists. We were all set for the wedding of the year.

Outside the church there was a sea of mulleted men in grey suits smoking, and women with shoulder pads, hats and white handbags. Everyone loved a wedding. It was a chance to get dolled up *Dallas* and *Dynasty* style and emulate royalty and celebrities and imagine for just one day that we could have a slice of that glamorous world. The excess of the 80s came into its own at weddings and in contrast to previous decades they were getting really showy. Even a low-key wedding like Miss McCoughney's was starting to sneak in elements of what we had watched on TV.

Miss McCoughney looked radiant and happy as she walked down the aisle towards Mr Roberts in her hooped ruffled dress of shiny white satin with large bows on the sleeves and bodice. Like many 80s brides she had taken inspiration from Princess Diana's dress. She had a huge floral wreath on her head and was accompanied by her dad (the Wimpy-buying hero), her sisters, channelling Southern belles in coral-hooped skirts, rosettes and swags, and two startled-looking pageboys in sailor suits. For the wedding photos she had too many silver plastic horseshoes on her arm to count. I must have used up an entire roll of film taking pictures of her, I just hoped that they would come out OK; severed heads, blurred figures and red eyes were usual for a novice photographer.

After the ceremony we all travelled to the local social club, which had been swagged everywhere in shiny white satin, and there were plastic pillars and brightly coloured silk flowers cascading everywhere you looked. The beautiful rose and carnation centrepieces were offset by plastic ashtrays at every table, which in a matter of hours would be overflowing. Everyone commented on how classy and beautiful the room was and unmarried females like myself made mental notes on the décor. Along with a DJ, who offered a running commentary in between pop songs and power ballads, multi-coloured strobe lights bouncing around the sticky dance floor, and a mostly beige buffet, this was a typical wedding in the 1980s.

All around the dance floor and propping up the bar in a haze of Benson & Hedges smoke were the men. Dancing around handbags on the dance floor were the women, and running and skidding between the two groups like escaped prisoners pursued by invisible guards were the children. This was because men, with the exception of Mr Gray, who seemed to be auditioning for *Saturday Night Fever*, didn't dance unless they were very drunk and then their wives would make them go home early. Instead, men lounged on chairs with their legs akimbo, smoking, drinking pints, eating pork pies and peanuts and talking about football. They would be made to dance with their wives, slow style, immediately after the bride and groom's first dance and then they had to sit back down.

It was not really socially acceptable for men to dance at weddings. Nightclubs, yes, because that was a courtship ritual, but weddings were a definite no-no. Besides, the courtship ritual was done and dusted by then – no need to get up from a seated position when music was played ever again. Of course I use the word dance in the vaguest sense of the word, because for most women dancing at weddings consisted of a kind of slow shuffle from one foot to another while rooted to the spot. The arms would be rigid, in a kind of boxing stance, probably ready to take on their husbands if they dared do something as embarrassing as wobble onto the dancefloor, pint in hand. The only exception to this wedding shuffle was when the novelty action song came on, then you could really go wild. Sometimes you could sit on the floor and pat it with your hand or sometimes you could mime spraying deodorant or ringing a bell. Sometimes you could be really imaginative and create your own move to the song lyrics. Oh yes, the 80s' wedding party was an absolute riot! Which is why it was always best to be a child at one, because you could skid across the floor as many times as you liked and no one would reprimand you, or failing that you could simply run round and round after the object of your affection until your face was bright red, and you were nearly sick, then you could go in search of some E numbers or discarded beer until you were ready to go back and start all over again!

A few hours later I had already chased Matthew Connelly several times around the club and he had chased me back. I'd had several breaks in between this to jump up and down manically with my friends to 'Star Trekkin' and 'The Chicken Song' and we had mimed putting deckchairs up our noses and beheading Eskimos to much hysterical laughter. We had then filled ourselves with beige delights from the buffet table, which was made even more perfect as Clyde Clancy had appointed himself buffet monitor to make sure there were plenty of vol-au-vents and fairy cakes left for us and there were no moms supervising to make sure we had a sandwich first.

As it got late and people started to get cabs home the DJ put on the power ballads. Caz, who had borrowed her mother's yellow stilettos for the party, took this as her opportunity to see if she could bag one of the boys to slow dance with her. Eventually Tony did the honours, even though she towered over him in her three-inch heels and looked like she was his mom shielding him from some tragedy. Then the best thing happened when Matthew Connelly asked me to dance with him! I was so excited I was almost sick. The evening ended with me swaying and leaning against Matthew's chest to the sound of Bonnie Tyler, and laughing at the boys in the rest of my class doing Kung Fu while trying to stretch Miss McCoughney's garter round their heads. I remember thinking life doesn't get any better than this.

Secondary School is an Anti-Climax

The problem with being in a relationship when you are ten or eleven years old is that it actually sucks. For about five minutes it's a status symbol because you actually have a boyfriend and feel like your life is sorted, but then comes the responsibility and routine and that's when it stops being fun.

Matthew Connelly had been my boyfriend for almost a week and I was already dreading going to school. I hated being the subject of gossip, I hated having to be so aware of how I looked as all my classmates were always staring at one or both of us so they could either report back to the others or take the piss. I also hated the way that Matthew Connelly monopolised breaktimes and dinnertimes so that we could have some time to ourselves, which meant invariably that he wanted to kiss me. I couldn't go and hang out with Ruth and my other friends and swap Garbage Pail Kids cards or play British Bulldog. Instead, I was expected to hang out in the cloakroom while Matthew told me he loved me and attempted to kiss me on the mouth like a starving goldfish while I leaned as far back as I could to escape it, muttering something about someone needing to clean paintbrushes. The social isolation, staring and piss-taking was the equivalent of having leprosy and I wanted out. So after about a week I arranged to swap him for some bubblegum and a deeley bopper headband in the shape of alien antennae. It was a bargain. I would have loved to have seen his face when he was hovering in the cloakroom and Caz showed up instead of me.

It was bittersweet when it was our last term at St Anthony's and soon Tony and I would be leaving and going to secondary school. As much as we wanted to grow up, leaving the security of our small Catholic primary school was going to be a wrench. Some of our friends were coming with us and some, like Ruth, were heading to grammar school. What was certain was that life was going to change dramatically. The comfort blanket that was our 80s childhood was coming to an end and a sea of strict school rules, dark uniforms and increasing self-reliance loomed before us. We would have given anything to have held onto teachers who were pseudo-parents, and Mr Proud's good work sweets at the end of a long week.

Secondary school was the biggest shock of my life. I had often heard Miss McCoughney refer to it as such when she said, 'You lot are going to have the biggest shock of your lives when you get to secondary school!' as she flung the blackboard rubber in frustration at one of our heads. We used to think she was being a bit over-dramatic and emotional. It turns out we had been mollycoddled in our little Catholic primary school for years, and our heads had been filled with too much *Grange Hill.* Although our secondary school had many comparable characters, it was none of the fun of the tea-time show we had grown to love.

Gone was the maternal warmth and good humour of our primary school. It was replaced by a more serious tribe of teachers who didn't seem to like us very much. They shouted a lot, were obsessed with rules and they regarded not having done your homework, or forgetting an item of your horrible PE kit as being akin to a criminal act, to be punished by handing out detentions, writing lines or being bawled at in front of your mates. I reckon that's why most of the girls started comfort eating. It was the shock. We had lost our school 'parents' so we found solace in homemade bread rolls slathered in butter, chocolate concrete and cream cakes which were waiting for us with open arms in the canteen each breaktime and at lunch. Physically we grew quickly, although not always in the right places.

I heard that the boys' school round the corner, where Tony had been sent, was no better. After school we would hurry home and sit on the kitchen worktop to compare tales of weird children, awful teachers and plans of rebellion as we scoffed entire packs of Garibaldi biscuits and milkshakes that we made with Nesquik powder. By this time our mom had progressed from her Open University course and was a history undergraduate at Birmingham Uni and we were coming home to an empty kitchen most nights.

On Thursdays we enjoyed a proper home-cooked meal when Nanny Pearl would come over to cook and tackle the ironing. She did this with an increased sense of purpose and vigour, going as far as sewing up the purposely positioned rips in our jeans and ironing creases down the centre of them. We were as baffled and embarrassed by this as she was by us. 'You used to be such smart children,' she lamented as she prised the Brosette bottle tops off my school brogues and carried them to the recycling corner. 'Now you both need to go to a fashion house to teach you how to dress!'

The truth was that now our lives were dominated by conformity and rules these small statements of fashion were about us asserting our individuality and independence (even if we all chose the same fashion statements and looked identical!).

After a few weeks a friend and I decided that we had had enough of the authoritarian approach of our new school so we decided we would go to the boys' school instead. We tied our hair back, borrowed some of the boys' spare uniform and off we went. No plan exactly, we just wanted a day off and to see how the other half lived. At first it was fun. We caused a bit of a stir as we strolled through the corridors. The noise levels were higher than in our school and there were definitely more bags and bodies being flung about, both accidentally and on purpose. Everywhere we turned there were boys flailing about, tripping, skidding, and sometimes rolling like beetles on their backs where they had been toppled by another in a display of bravado. It also smelled more than our school. Our school smelled of hairspray and cabbage. This place smelled stuffy like earth and damp, with canteen cabbage thrown in. No wonder, I felt, did the boys appear to be falling over. They were knocked out by the smell! We took our places quietly in the back of the class. No one dared grass us up.

The morning passed uneventfully. The English teacher, aged, solemn-faced and weary, rarely looked up from the book of Yeats' poetry he was discussing in a monotone voice. I began to feel invincible and excited that my true guise was undiscovered, especially as I loved English literature and poetry. I could not resist making an enthusiastic contribution to the lesson when the teacher was dissecting a verse called 'The Second Coming'. I felt that the 'ceremony of innocence' referred to in it was about baptism and put my hand up and said so. The teacher looked me straight in the eye and said, 'Yes, you could be right,' before looking back down again to roars of background laughter, and counting the days until he could retire.

We managed to keep the guise up until lunchtime, when the news of our outing reached the boys' teachers. They were very kind to us and said that we must have lost our way. They then let us eat our lunch in the staff room before driving us back to the girls' school where our head of year was not kind to us at all and screamed until we thought the blood vessels in her eyes would pop. How we hated our school and its strictness. I could not wait to leave. The contempt of many of the teachers towards us was mutual and it was unclear who was to blame for this unsatisfactory situation. It was like the chicken and egg scenario. No one would ever know which group had given up their enthusiasm first.

I remembered with fondness how Mr Proud and Miss McCoughney had gleefully allowed us to 'soak the teacher' and chuck wet sponges at them while they sat in the stocks at St Anthony's charity events. I missed those days. However, I was as determined as most of my friends to make the best of a bad situation and we would have fun however we could while we were there.

From what I could gather, the teacher-pupil relationship wasn't much better in Tony's school.

Vinny Thompson, the worst-behaved kid there, actually tried to blow the boys' and the girls' schools up. He had planned it for ages. One Saturday night, he broke in (no alarms, no CCTV, no double-glazing in schools in those days, so getting in was the easy part). He ran up to the science labs and attached and turned on all the Bunsen burners, left them on and arrived triumphant at the park to say that if we all went and catapulted lit cigarettes through the science lab windows both schools would be blasted into the sky. How we all cheered when we heard! Despite the best efforts of a few enthusiastic volunteers, both schools were still there when Monday morning rolled around, much to our disappointment.

My girls' school, which still clung to its 1950s' values. The teachers had a very irritating habit of calling us 'ladies' rather than 'girls' or 'children' or simply 'class', as in 'Now ladies it is time to get out your cooking ingredients.'

The school was in a time warp. Some may say this was commendable, as traditional values and decorum crumbled around us. I just found it embarrassing as I lugged my compulsory home economics basket with gingham cloth like a demented Dorothy past the boys' school. There was simply no way I was ever going to get a boyfriend if I looked like someone's gran!

There was a plaque in reception celebrating all the notable achievements of former pupils. The plaque was mostly blank except for the mention of a former 'lady' who had featured in *Good Housekeeping*, and someone who became Personal Assistant to a local MP. At Tony's school the achievements plaque in their reception took up an entire wall! The fallen and victorious of two World Wars, solicitors, barristers, local MPs, someone that was on *Blockbusters* – the programme, not the video rental chain. I wished I had the nerve to engrave, 'I'll have an S please, Bob' next to it. 'S is for Sexist!'

I found it very difficult to get my head round why our school plaque could not have been a bit more impressive. Our school was over a hundred years old. Its former pupils had seen two world wars, our Prime Minister was female and surely someone had achieved a professional qualification somewhere along the way! After all, Nanny Pearl had been a land girl in the Second World War, most of her friends had done their bit in the Auxiliary Territorial Service or one of the forces, and lots of women had been to university in the previous decades.

There was no way that all the schools' former pupils could have missed a century of world events because they were sitting at home waiting to boil the perfect egg. I decided to voice my concern to our head teacher by letter. I was summoned to a very angry meeting which consisted of my class teacher, my head of year and the head. All of them sensibly permed, skirt-suited and wearing beige tights, wearing slapped-face expressions. After a brief lecture I was ordered to follow the rules, not to question the school's decisions and to write an essay on, 'The Importance of Doing as You are Told'. I felt very angry and humiliated and I would be writing no such essay. I prayed for a humour injection into my school to lighten the atmosphere and make the teachers crack a smile.

I was always in trouble at school for questioning the rules; whether it was asking why we could not learn more useful subjects such as car maintenance and woodwork, to refusing to write an assignment on the 'emotions' I felt about the knitted individual squares my class had just been made to do. I felt fenced in by my gender and disappointed by the expectation to conform. Our little suburban area needed to catch up with the changes that were going on in places like London and New York. Girls could do anything boys could by the late 80s if *Cosmopolitan* magazine was to be believed. They had 'power dressing' and geometric blusher. Besides, I thought as I surveyed my attempt at a knitted wool square, if anyone feels emotion towards a piece of wool then surely they need professional help, not a gold star sticker. I was not backward in coming forward and explaining my point, and besides, my 'knitting' resembled a colander that had been steam-rolled and then put through a shredder. So the only emotion I could have remotely experienced was what I wrote down in my exercise-book, 'feeling grateful for high-street knitwear'. My teachers didn't see the funny side.

My prayers were answered in 1988 in the form of the first Comic Relief. No one had ever seen a charity event like it before, my school was no exception. The whole country was getting involved. Up until this point my teachers' idea of charity fundraising was a sponsored silence or a sponsored walk. The concept of doing something funny to raise money for charity, to wear a clown's nose or fancy dress for the day, was going to be a proposition that no school in the country was getting out of. Slowly but surely the ideas and the smiles began to creep into the classroom. Perhaps we could all dress in silly costumes, including the teachers? How about hosting an *It's a Knockout* day in the field with relay races and daft challenges? Even the Royal Family had moved with the times and done something like this.

For weeks the school buzzed with excitement and ideas. To our surprise, most of our teachers began to share our enthusiasm. They were persuaded to wear fancy dress, (with the exception of the PE teachers who had some kind of gene that made them sadistic).

When Comic Relief day arrived I happily met my group of friends in the St Trinian's uniform and roller skates ensembles that we had decided would be the funniest things to wear, but not before I had crashed into several garages when my wheels took on a life of their own during the shortcut I used to take each morning. I finally met my clones on the corner where they were wobbling on their skates. The idea hadn't really been based on humour at all. It was just an excuse to dress like our idol, Madonna, for the day and get away with it. Fishnet tights, full make-up, short skirts and bras peeking over the top of our open blouses. We though we looked like the sexiest things since one of her pop videos. The roller skate addition was just so we could whizz past the boys' school in a sleek and cool manner and hope that they would stop and stare longingly at the sexy girls rushing past.

We finally arrived at school after a few detours. Firstly we had to remove someone in the gang from a privet hedge where she'd landed head first, wheels still spinning mid-air. Secondly we were pursued by Spiderman, Jimmy Savile wielding a giant inflatable cigar, and Zippy from *Rainbow,* ending up in someone's flower bed in a disorganised rugby scrum as we weren't quite as sleek on wheels as we had thought.

School was great that day. Staff and pupils had conversations, laughed at each other and played games. Most importantly money was raised for a good cause. The next day it was as if it had never happened but it showed us that most of our teachers were at least human. I may never learn to boil an egg or knit a square but at least somewhere within those teachers was the possibility that they might be able to laugh about it. The legacy of the very first Comic Relief was to confirm to British society that having a sense of humour in your day-to-day life, regardless of your age or social class, was not only acceptable but commendable. Furthermore if you could raise money for charity at the same time, even better. From then on wacky fundraising became mainstream; from people sitting in baths full of baked beans, to impersonating social and geographical stereotypes. It was just before political correctness emerged and everyone had to mind their 'Ps' and 'Qs', but for most of the 80s, ignorance was often bliss.

Linda Lusardi Lives With Benny Hill

Grandad Jimmy always used to buy *The Sun* newspaper and the *News of The World* on a Sunday, then sit reading it for hours completely switched off from the world around him. I especially loved the *News of the World* supplement which was imaginatively called '*Sun Day*'. It was absolutely my favourite magazine before I got into boys and fashion. Grandad Jimmy never read it. It's just as well as if he had I don't think he would have felt it was suitable literature for a young girl.

Sun Day was one of the most sexist magazines that ever existed. There was always relationship advice for married women, which often revolved around spicing up your marriage by dressing as a schoolgirl along with some photos of 'Page 3' girls bent over a table showing you how it should be done while multi-tasking making a family casserole and hanging out washing. There were also quite often entertaining quizzes along the lines of, 'Are you a Missus or a Mistress?' with a photo of a wife looking mighty pissed off while scrubbing the floor and the 'mistress' having lots of fun, laughing, drinking champagne and taking delivery of a new car, while dressed in fishnets and a fur coat. If you scored low you were a 'Missus' and were scolded in the results and told to dress up as a schoolgirl more. If you were a home-wrecker you were told

'Congratulations! Keep up the good work! Remember not to talk too much,' or something like that.

There was also a problem page where men apparently wrote in every week and complained about accidentally 'shagging' their wife's sexy sister or were worried about the size of their 'manhood'. It was always referred to as a 'manhood' and I used to think if the man really had genuine concern about it why on earth would he write to a women's magazine to tell them about it? As for the affairs, the men always received sympathy from the 'female' agony aunt, which is why it is perfectly obvious now that the entire magazine was written by men. If the agony aunt had been a real female she would have organised a lynch mob to seek out the sister-in-law 'shagger' and slice off his micro-penis.

There would also be revealing articles about the amazing lives of the rich and famous which readers, myself amongst them, lapped up and believed to be absolutely true, but that of course were entirely fabricated. Some of them outrageously so as I realised when I found some back issues recently. Amongst them was a guide to adopting George Best's superior lifestyle and fitness schedule (with no mention of week-long benders and new livers), Boy George's quest for a baby, the 'truth', about George Michael and all his girlfriends, and my personal favourite, 'A day in the life of Linda Lusardi', which involved her doing a bit of housework in a bra and knickers, then going to work and doing a glamour shoot before going home and serving up dinner to some lecherous Benny Hill type bloke who just happened to live in her house. The crazy thing was, readers like myself were so gullible we couldn't get enough of it.

Ruth and Celia, used to mock my reading habits and refer

to the men that wrote such things as 'male chauvinist pigs'. After a while Ruth got so fed up of the sight of the *Sun Day* magazine sticking out of my school bag (I had to phone Mystic Meg's horoscope line from the phone box every Monday) that she reduced the feminist arguments to simply making oinking noises every time I popped round for an after-school catch-up. Ruth had no chance of being a tabloid fan as, by the late 1980s, Celia had become a prominent campaigner for the Labour Party. She had made friends with a local MP named Clare Short, a highly intelligent woman with a dry sense of humour who used to pop into their house for coffee in her lunch breaks. Clare became a household name and tabloid punchbag when she launched an unsuccessful campaign to get Page 3 girls banned. She claimed it was degrading to women. It sexualised them and trivialised their roles. In a time when the tabloids frequently described women as 'busty' or 'bimbos' in the introductory paragraphs of any news stories about them, she was fighting a losing battle. She was labelled 'fat' and 'jealous' for her campaign and one time her car got egged in protest while we were all sitting enjoying a fair trade coffee and discussing cat names for Ruth's new kitten (I was in favour of 'Garfield' but they settled on 'Desmond Tutu').

I admired Clare Short a lot, but I wouldn't want to be her, I thought as she drove off with egg sliding down her windscreen. To be considered 'outspoken' or a 'feminist' was the equivalent of being put in the stocks back in medieval times. I would never be that brave. I did tell Grandad Jimmy however that his newspaper was offensive to women. He hadn't noticed, (he said), he bought it because at least he had a chance of finishing the crosswords.

Clare Short's campaign was way ahead of its time. The prewar chivalry of my grandparents' era was by then virtually obliterated and from its cinders snaked something sinister, which was rapidly becoming regarded as normal: the socially tolerated pervert. The sexualisation of women had become so normalised through the tabloid press that young women and girls needed to be protected.

I don't think we heard the word paedophile in the 80s. It was a very naïve time. It is hard to believe now, but back then, it seemed much more acceptable for men to sleep with girls aged under sixteen. Now they put men behind bars for this but in the 80s, if a girl looked like a woman, she was considered fair game, regardless of her actual age. Some teenage celebrities built successful careers around getting into nightclubs, drinking and having relationships with famous older men, and one celebrity tennis player actually boasted in the tabloids about the mother of his son being a thirteen-year-old schoolgirl. With these sorts of messages being thrown at people by the media, it is easy to see now why paedophilia was tolerated and even indirectly encouraged. They say there's a sex offender on every street; well, back in the 80s, they were not only on every street but in parks, pubs, and on pavements openly advertising themselves with pride.

Something that myself and other girls used to encounter quite often in the 80s was the flasher. This was a man who liked to silently flash his privates at women and then go about his business as if nothing had happened, leaving a shocked and often panicky female behind. There was a really shy one at Rowheath Park who used to just take Polaroids of his bits and leave them pinned to trees for people to find. We found this hilarious and used to keep them to pin on the backs of people we knew if we became bored. I don't think this was quite the flasher's intention though, the intention was usually to shock and distress. The stereotype of the flasher was the old social misfit in a long mac but in reality they came in all age groups and there was no overcoat uniform. I have no idea what happened to flashers since that decade, they seem to be extinct now. Maybe they are now the types that frequent online dating sites and send unsolicited photos of their 'dicks' for their own gratification.

To illustrate the laissez-faire attitude to the paedophile and the voyeur, I remember an elderly guy who lived a few doors up from my school. Every home time he would stand outside his front door and watch the girls walk past while simultaneously rummaging in his trouser pocket. He was a well- known local character who everyone said was 'harmless' on account of his age and the fact that he was apparently a war veteran. Well I didn't think he was harmless. He was always ready to dole out cigarettes to which-ever girl craved one, in return for them bending over and pulling up a few weeds from his front garden. After a while I was getting quite sick of observing this so after seeking advice from Celia Payne I decided to organise a petition to give the girls the right to wear trousers for their own safety. Despite gaining many signatures, our head and deputy head teachers, who loved their traditional girls' school, shot me down and told me that not only was my idea ridiculous but I was making unfounded allegations against an elderly member of the community which had apparently reached his attention and he was most offended. I was told to take him a present of something beautiful to compensate for my disrespectful statements. Of course I did as I was told and so the next day promptly egg and floured his house. I had always found beauty in baking. We didn't see much of him after that.

Teenage Dating

The pursuit of true love was a hobby for me and most of my school friends in the 80s. Valentine's Day was probably the most important day in the calendar if you were a teenager. This was the day when you found out if all your efforts to get noticed by anyone at the boys' school had actually worked.

As soon as the cards hit the shelves in Hallmark Cards in Cotteridge we would be in there after school. You couldn't move for teenage girls agonising over whether to buy the humorous one, the one with the sex references or the cute one with the fat teddy bear on the front. It was a huge dilemma. We also gazed longingly at the top shelf in the card shop which displayed the most expensive cards for the people who really meant business. The enormous A3-sized cards, the padded ones and the ones that played a tune when you opened them were for people that were really in love, maybe even at the 'let's get eternitised' stage, which was the teenage equivalent of getting engaged.

The shop owner, a Mr Bunn, had placed the expensive cards well out of the reach of our grubby hands. He was a proper old-school salesman but he had unbecoming delusions of grandeur. If he liked you, he called you 'sir' or 'madam' and you got shown the exclusive range of top shelf cards, and overpriced 'Forever

Friends' teddies with their bow ties and inflated price tags, especially if you happened to be wearing a suit. His shop, I once overheard him say, was on the classy side of the street sandwiched between the greengrocers and Braggs the Bakers, with the 'common side' opposite with its 'Moneysavers' bargain shop where you could buy cut-glass vases for fifty pence and multi-packs of everything from perfume to knickers. He never sold charity cards, he used to tell the speechless reps that came in, but his conscience was eased as he had once put 'a whole ten-pound note in a Christian Aid envelope'. His shop and its goods, he believed, attracted a 'better clientele', which was why hordes of school kids choosing Valentine's Day cards were an inconvenience to him, and why his hawk-eyed wife used to eyeball us from behind the till like we were tramps that had wandered in off the street to keep warm.

Mr Bunn never missed a day's work and always dressed smartly with a pullover stretched over his large tummy and a shirt and bow tie. He was an embodiment of the soft toys he sold. He took enormous pride in his cards, mugs and key-rings as though they were Fabergé eggs and was constantly polishing, straightening and gazing lovingly upon them as he strolled up and down the two aisles. I didn't like to line his pockets with anything, but within his shop were the only gifts that my friends and I really wanted, so a whole week worth of pocket money was lavished upon Valentine's cards that could say everything we wanted to declare without fear or ridicule. As for the top shelf cards, they were well out of our price range, but we dreamed of waking up to find an anonymous one by our front door, ideally with a single red rose. The 80s really was the decade of cringe when it came to romance.

My friend Jenny, who was thirteen like me, was in a relationship with a sixth-former. She was lucky enough to get the works: the fat teddies, the padded cards and even the much coveted 'eternity ring'. She didn't even have to 'do it' with him, much to the disbelief of the self-styled 'popular' girls in our class who believed that the best way to get noticed was to behave like someone five years older.

There was a much-loved booked called *Forever* by Judy Blume that did the rounds of most teenage girls' classrooms in the 1980s. It was always yellowed and dog-eared by all the eager reading it had endured. It was about a teenage girl and her boyfriend and their adventures in 'doing it' for the first time (and a few times after that). Like most of my contemporaries I read it in the confines of my bedroom of an evening and was both horrified and awed. I don't remember the characters, or the plot, only that the boy had a penis called 'Ralph' and it had a starring role. Many 80s girls learned some of the first things about sex from that book, usually well before they encountered the real thing. Such adult behaviour was something I was incapable of so I spent a large amount of class time doodling the name of my crush in hearts and arrows with the initials 'TLA' underneath (true love always) and 'IDST' (if destroyed still true) to emphasise how serious I was. I could have won a prize in daydreaming and wishing. I don't think I had thought through exactly how the object of my affection would enhance my life. Most boys my age were still half the size of us girls, wiry, awkward and spotty and had conversations limited to boasting about drunken exploits or near-misses with the law. They were nothing like the golden-haired, double-denim wholesome boys of our fantasies. I blame Stock Aitken Waterman and their fairy-tale hits.

The 'love letter' was another cringe-worthy relic from the 80s that is now extinct. Painstakingly hand-written by boyfriends and girlfriends, or the desperate to be noticed and slightly deranged. Written under the lights of bedside lamps after being grounded by parents, or separated by distance (and probably to the sound of Richard Marx on cassette), they were evidence of true love. I fantasised about receiving one myself, but the day one actually plonked onto the mat after school one day, instead of feeling flattered and delighted, I began to feel panicky and trapped.

Tony found it first. I'd been making the compulsory after-school Nesquiks and suddenly there he was waving a pink envelope in my face with a biro heart on it and the initials 'SWALK' (sealed with a loving kiss) scrawled across the back. I was equally amazed and mortified and I had to chase him round the house to retrieve it after he threatened to open it and read its contents aloud or else it was going in the microwave. I wanted to read it in private. I had no idea who could have sent it.

Later in my room after reading two pages of someone declaring undying love for me and asking if he could walk me to school, I began to feel anxious and sick. Having a secret admirer was nothing like I had imagined. It made me self-conscious and worried about leaving the house. It would have to be reported to my friends and advice must be sought.

The author of the letter was quickly identified and outed as a boy my age that lived opposite me. It didn't take long to find the wannabe Lothario out. There was always one over-loud and self-proclaimed 'in the know' girl who acted like a megaphone between the girls' and boys' schools. Apparently Lothario and his friends had spent an agonising hour in the school library debating over whether to start the letter with 'dear' 'darling' or 'sexy' and between them had assisted their friend to compose what in their opinion was just the right kind of romantic piece that a girl would want, along with sketched hearts and arrows.

Back at the girls' school, the agreed solution to the letter problem was that I should of course write the sender a love letter back saying how I would love him to walk me to school; after all, I should be flattered and consider myself lucky that I was on the receiving end of such a coveted token of admiration. My friends more or less composed the perfect romantic response back to him. I just signed it. I sensed the offence and disappointment I would cause if I didn't play along and so my journey to school was about to change.

I was mortified. I had hoped for a get-out-of-jail-free card, instead I now appreciated somewhat how people facing arranged marriages must feel. My friends were excited for me, presumed I felt the same giddy excitement that they did. They were probably already planning their bridesmaids' outfits.

For the next few days the Lothario called for me and walked me the painfully long way round to school. I couldn't think of a word to say to him so I just listened as he banged on about the plots of *Moonlighting* with Bruce Willis and Cybill Shepherd. Gosh he loved that show! All sixty-six episodes of it. I'd never even heard of it but by the end of that week I was experienced in zoning out whenever I heard the words 'Maddie and David', while painfully aware of the fact that my friends were giggling in the bushes behind us in the hope that they might just get to see us kissing.

Fast-forward to the end of the first week. I had really had enough. I was never reading *Just Seventeen* articles again. If this was what having a boyfriend was all about they could wipe their arses with it! I wanted out! I was fed up with the chore of daily love letters, I didn't want to hold anyone's hand and I missed my friends' goofy jokes on the way to school. I wanted to end it but I had no idea how. My mom said I should tell him to his face, but I would rather do a swimming gala in a shell suit. I decided to write it in the daily 'love letter'. Sensing my writer's block, after some hours agonising over a blank piece of paper, Tony volunteered to write it on my behalf. It was probably for the best, he wasn't emotionally involved and he could post it for me as well. I was grateful and relieved to hand the responsibility over to him.

The next day on our way home from school I noticed my ex's friends shaking their heads in dismay at me as we walked past them. I wasn't sure why but guessed that they, like my friends, were disappointed that love's young dream had come to an abrupt end.

However the truth was later revealed via the human mega-phone, that my final 'love letter' had consisted not of a subtly composed communication, gently suggesting the cessation of our relationship, but a large drawing of a cartoon penis, which is what you can expect when you ask your teenage brother to break up with your boyfriend for you. Lothario's pride wasn't hurt for too long though. I often saw him walking his latest girlfriend to school or leaving his house to post a pink envelope. He eventually became an English and drama teacher so all that early practice must have paid off.

Clubbing With Fake ID

It was relatively easy to obtain alcohol if you were underage. Even if you looked about five, fake ID could be easily made by putting your photo on an NUS card, doctoring the date of birth and photocopying it a few times so you became eighteen. If you were still suspected of being too young to drink you would only ever be asked your date of birth, and the fake one had always been memorised in readiness for the inevitable question. The shop worker or nightclub doorman, who had been daft enough to think they could catch you out with such an obvious question, would just shrug and say 'OK, in you go,' or 'do you want any cigarettes with that?' They must have surely known that we were underage. Quite often when we were drinking in our local nightclub we would hear the staff comment, 'Have you remembered your homework?' and we used to laugh. They didn't care. The police had better things to do than trawl establishments for under-age drinkers or pursue the dirty mac brigade. They were probably kept too busy in the pursuit of joyriders and serial killers who were peaking in society in the 1980s.

Mine and my friend's favourite nightclub when we were teenagers was called 'The Dome' and it was in Birmingham city centre. Most of us could get in by the time we were thirteen or fourteen. We used to go to the Tuesday student night as it was easier to get in, although we all had to all pretend to be staying at a friend's house for a homework project to get away with it. Tony couldn't get in when I first started going. He had to stay at home and play Pac-Man for a few years until he got hair on his face. It was harder for boys. Girls could just slap a bit of makeup on, put some socks in a bra if you didn't yet have anything to put in yours, hairspray your hair until it was stiff as a pencil and hey presto, we could be eighteen. I reckon most of the kids in 'The Dome' were school or sixth-form students.

The other advantage of going on a student night was that you could get pints of half lager, half cider, known as a 'snakebite' for a pound, which was within our budget, even if it was so watered down you had to have blackcurrant in it just to taste it.

Fortunately, you didn't need to dress up. Don't get me wrong, I would have loved to have dressed up like the real adult females in the nightclubs up town with their metallics and their bows, batting my khol-rimmed eyes and sipping something sophisticated out of a tiny glass but that would have meant having to tolerate real adult males with their pale suits, skinny ties and slip-on shoes and I wasn't ready for that scene yet. Like all the other underage drinkers in there we were in a nightclub to get out of the house for a bit and practise dancing like MC Hammer, fuelled by 'snakebite'. We certainly weren't there to look for a future partner for ourselves, that was Mystic Meg's job. So, our fashions were like those of the university students. It set us apart and gave us some protection, like a code. We were there to listen to the music and wobble around like lightweights, spilling pints on the sticky carpet, which was always *very* sticky. It was like walking on the moon in some clubs before the invention of laminate flooring.

As far as our fashions went the legs on our jeans were so wide we had to tuck them into our socks to stop tripping over them. The trainers on our feet were never laced up, the trainers themselves were padded out with socks at the front so they looked chunky. The effect was that of having giant branded hooves instead of feet. You couldn't even walk normally in them. You ended up doing some kind of odd half-zombie walk, which combined with the suction of the carpet meant that no one ever fell over after having one too many. You never saw the slipping and sliding around and landing on backsides that you see so often in drinking establishments today.

My friend Ruth immersed herself with more intellectual grammar-school types than I was lumbered with at my all girls' comprehensive. Ruth, who was never one for conforming to popular fashion, had become a goth. She and her new friends wore long black tasselled skirts, baggy tops and black lipstick. They went to moodier clubs like 'Edwards Number 7' and listened to alternative music. They looked like packs of depressed crows. Occasionally I would bump into Ruth at 'The Dome' where she spent the night in a special Goth side room with other deep-thinking people, probably thinking about vampires and 'The Cure'. Once, I went in to find her and I felt like the odd one out at a Halloween Party. I didn't stay there long. Everyone looked at me like I'd escaped from a neon mental asylum. My smiley face acid hoodie was clearly offending those for whom smiling was banned. I went back to the dance floor in the main club and jumped around manically like I didn't have a care in the world.

It didn't take long for Tony to grass me up to our parents. He was only jealous but I had to put a hold on the Tuesday night homework sessions for a few years. Until then I was under close scrutiny so I would need to be quite creative if I wanted to get any freedom.

Fad Diets and Expanding People

One of the most immediately noticeable things about my secondary school was the size of some of the girls. Probably one in three of them was overweight; some of them took up so much space that they had to have showers on their own because if they came in with the rest of us it would have been sexual assault. There was one, Carly Trueman, who used her weight to win arguments and was notorious for sitting on girls whom she disagreed with, or any that she felt had given her what she thought was a dirty look. Most of us feared her but she was popular because no one dared disagree with her. To witness an argument she was involved in was like watching someone get obliterated by a bomb made out of dough. When a gang of teachers hoisted her off her victim you always half-expected to see a chalk outline where the body had been. Her biggest brag was that she had once openly swiped an entire crate of hairspray from her local shop and when the shopkeeper gave chase she had simply sat on him until he wheezed and spluttered that she could keep it, an event that she felt gave her some higher status and a reputation as 'hard'.

I had never seen obesity so frequently before and I don't think anyone else had either. The surge of enormous teenagers was the result of many families taking the convenience food trend of the early 80s too far. This, combined with the advent of cable TV, MTV and more time spent staring at the screen, school dinners with no restrictions on the amount of cream cakes, chips and chocolate concrete you could purchase for break-times and dinner, led to the inevitable consequence of 'lardy kids'. Mind you, some of the parents were no better and a lot of adults were starting to rapidly expand too.

Grandad Jimmy used to feel quite sad about the size of people, especially women, and used to lament over the 1950s silhouette, something that was threatening to become extinct.

'You never see them any more, normal ones walking around,' he used to say wistfully when we walked through Cotteridge after I demanded he chaperone me home after school so I didn't have to face the indignity of walking past the boys' school alone. I got mercilessly teased about my elderly companion but I didn't care. One inappropriate comment towards me from any boy and my grandad, who had survived the D-Day landings, would have hoisted them up and thrown them over the nearest fence if I had wanted him to.

'What are you talking about Grandad?' I would ask and he would cautiously nudge me and indicate a shell-suited young mother waddling behind a pushchair, portion of chips in one hand and pushchair handle and fag in the other.

Even my dad was starting to fear that the fat epidemic was going to invade our house and was starting to eye my mother suspiciously as she sat doing her university essays. He told her to be careful not to sit down too long otherwise her bum would get big. Sometimes he would hover outside the dining room and stare at her hunched over her books as if he were expecting her to suddenly turn into Bella Emberg. My mom would shout at him for his misogynistic remarks.

As a response to the nationally expanding waistlines, dieting started to become a pastime with a lot of women. Most women tried at least one fad diet during this time in an attempt to become like the spandex-clad aerobics stars on the TV, with their tiny belts round their leotards.

Some women, like my mom's friend Jean, were not overweight but became consumed with the idea that they were, and dieting became an obsession. Every time I overheard Jean talking to my mom there was some new diet she was raving about. From Weight Watchers, to Slimfast, to cottage cheese. You name the diet, that woman had tried it. Once she spent an entire morning trying to convince my mom to try something called the Cabbage Soup Diet and glorified its benefits.

'All you need to do is eat cabbage soup three times a day for breakfast, lunch and dinner. It's so easy, Teresa, and I've never felt so good. I've stuck to it for the past four days, you should try it,' she raved enthusiastically while breaking open the fourth can of Diet Coke she always kept stored under her kid's pushchair (calorie-free, which meant she could indulge as often as she liked).

'What else can you eat?' asked my mom while pulling a secret vomiting face to me when Jean's back was turned.

'What else?' said Jean in shock as if it were the most ridiculous question ever asked.

'You don't need anything else. It's so healthy, why would you need anything else? Well you can drink as many Diet Cokes as you like so you won't miss sugar.' She knocked her head back without stopping for breath, glug, glug, glug, before putting the can in the bin and opening another one.

'You have nothing to lose by giving it a go! Just think you can be the same size as Bridget Fonda by the weekend and that would stop Alan commenting about the size of your backside!'

My mother looked unsure but Jean was wide-eyed and insistent. My mother wouldn't be swayed though. It didn't sound very appetising, and besides, she didn't believe that crash diets worked. If you wanted to lose weight then lifestyle changes and exercise was the best way forward, along with reading *The Vitamin Bible* which had been lent to her by Celia Payne.

Jean never exercised, unless you counted pushing a pram full of Diet Coke up to St Anthony's school at what seemed like thirty miles an hour and back again. Within minutes it seemed the pair of them had arranged to go 'walking' that evening to Rowheath Park and back.

By 7pm Mom was in the hall dressed in my dad's Pierre Cardin tracksuit, complete with a towelling headband which Tony and I found hilarious. Jean called for her clad in hot pink spandex leggings with shorts over the top, pink towelling head band and matching wrist bands and leg warmers. This was not an unusual sight for the time. We watched bemused as Jean jogged on the spot on the doorstep while waiting for Mom to put her trainers on. Then off they went, half speed-walking, half jogging down the road with us waving them off.

Around thirty minutes later she was back, red in the face, staggering and breathing heavily. When she collapsed onto the sofa she told us it hadn't gone so well. Apparently the downside of the Cabbage Soup Diet was that it made you shit, a lot. When combined with several litres of caffeine and a jog round your local park the result is catastrophic, as poor Jean discovered when her insides threatened to rebel while she was doing a half-sprint around the duck pond. With no public toilets nearby and only seconds to spare, she ended up squatting over the pond to relieve herself with my mom not knowing whether to do star jumps to distract people or keep running and pretend she was on a solo outing. She settled for standing in a nearby bush and laughing her head off. Needless to say she and Jean never went jogging again!

The 'Foreign Holiday'

By 1989 my mom had made enough money from hosting English language students for us to venture into the unknown and we booked our first package holiday to Spain. The package holiday brochures looked so enticing. They were all sun, golden beaches, and ecstatic looking families, holding hands and frolicking in clear blue waters. I had never met any families that actually all held hands like paper dolls in public but seemingly this is what a foreign holiday did to people. My parents were sold.

My dad point blank refused to fly there due to all the plane crashes and hijackings that seemed to frequent the news at that time. Also, he had watched way too many of the increasingly popular human disaster movies that seemed to spin off from world affairs and feed the public imagination and desire for gory details. He was not going on a plane ever again and that was that. My mom was quite happy to fly but my dad went into overdrive, pacing up and down the kitchen and relaying tales of all the dreadful things that could happen to us if we did. Within a week I'd listened to various scenarios, from us hanging limply onto a plane wing while bobbing in the ocean and being slowly eaten by sharks, to being manhandled out of the plane door mid-flight by men with guns and balaclavas so it was decided that we would travel there by coach. My mom had a condition of her own. Grandad Jimmy and Nanny Pearl were coming along too.

The great day came and we boarded the Sunseekers' coach in Birmingham city centre with all the other families, most of whom were also novice travellers who had taken advantage of the new cheap package deals and the promise of better weather and harmonious family experiences rather than a traditional English break. Plus, it gave people a bit of status if they could take their annual holidays abroad and that was worth risking a dodgy tummy and going without a decent cup of tea for. Nanny Pearl had never been abroad before and had never planned to but now it was becoming more popular she was keen to see what all the fuss was about. Grandad hadn't been abroad since he was de-mobbed in 1945 but he'd never had a holiday abroad either, so it was a first for all of us. To be honest we couldn't wait. We'd seen the brochure and there were outdoor water parks there, which was something we didn't have at home, and the holiday couldn't come soon enough.

Mom and Nanny Pearl packed a separate suitcase just for food. There had been rumours that the supermarkets in Spain were very odd. You could search all morning for familiar items for a beach picnic and all you would find were endless bumper bags of crisps with funny names, a studded cucumber and a miniature loaf of overpriced bread that tasted like it had been rolled in sugar. Eating out at one of the many pavement cafés, with their checked plastic tablecloths, suited waiters and lobster tanks (you chose one and they boiled them alive) was a far easier option, even if everything was doused in chips. Failing that just take a suitcase of baked beans, teabags, bread, cornflakes and corned beef and mealtimes would be just like being at home.

A few hours later we were on the *Pride of Free Enterprise* listening to our parents having an argument over Dad's decision to dye his grey hair dark brown in readiness for the holiday. Nanny and Grandad decided to take us up on deck to get some air. I remembered how I had attempted to dye my own hair auburn, like Belinda Carlisle's, with Harmony temporary hair tint. When I emerged from the bathroom, looking like a traffic cone, I got a right telling off. Cheap hair dye just seemed to be something that irritated my mom a lot. She would be fine in a few hours.

As we stood on the deck of the ferry and watched Dover's white cliffs get smaller and smaller Grandad Jimmy told me the last time he had seen them, he and his friends didn't know if they would ever see them again, and for a moment he was lost in his thoughts. I knew from whispers between my mom and Nanny Pearl that out of the cheeky-faced group of young lads in berets and khaki in the photo he kept in his room, he was the only one who came back. He used to go back there sometimes when something reminded him and I knew better than to ask him poorly timed questions. He was back in 1989 as soon as Nanny Pearl started shouting excitedly that she'd spotted a dolphin and a seal and started winding her camera up, but it turned out to be a carrier bag and an old tyre.

It was a long, cramped and stuffy journey and by the time we got off the ferry at Calais and started the second leg of the drive through France and towards the Pyrenees we started to wish we had left our dad at home and flown. France was not all quaint historic villages and people riding bikes in berets but just as dirty, noisy and full of grey tower blocks as the cities back home. Plus, it smelled badly of sewage and when we stopped off for snacks and to stretch our legs we found to our horror that many public toilets were in fact a hole in the ground, which made our primary school toilet hut at St Anthony's seem like a stately home.

We were expected to sleep through the night on the coach in a seated position. Even with a pillow, the choice of the window or the back of a rigid seat to rest your weary head upon was frustratingly uncomfortable, and so neck-cramp-inducing that you just wanted to kick the hell out of the seat in front, or even better, press the emergency button and start hitch-hiking back home. Tony and I reluctantly stayed up all night. By the time we reached the Pyrenees the next morning I swear I'd had a skin breakout from the stress. My dad was the only one who said he'd had the most refreshing sleep when we started moaning at him. He said he felt fresh as a daisy. He was lying of course, which was pretty obvious when he stepped off the coach to get the drinks in and with an exaggerated sprightly step went straight through what he thought was the café entrance and straight into a French toilet right foot first.

It was a bit concerning and rather alien arriving in Spain for the first time. I was alarmed to see how very un-green it was compared to home. Instead of lush green fields, their countryside seemed to consist of vast expanses of dusty land with parched and scratchy-looking greenery poking out of it. There were a lot of concrete walls everywhere, some were painted white and some were covered in graffiti and words I did not understand. I hoped it would be different when we got to the Costa Brava. I missed home already and maybe another caravan holiday in Aberystwyth wouldn't have been so bad after all.

By the afternoon the buildings were starting to look whiter and cleaner and we caught our first glimpse of the sea. What a sight it was. The water was so vibrant and blue and sparkly, unlike the churning grey sea we were used to at home. Suddenly, I had waves of excitement and adventure in my tummy and when I looked at Tony and saw he had perked up, I knew he was feeling the same way. This was going to be no ordinary holiday. This was going to be fun!

The Costa Brava in the 1980s was just starting to get invaded by hordes of British tourists and it was beginning to adapt. Every pavement was littered with small tables, chairs, ashtrays, and sandwich boards with photographs of food to tempt us in; sausage and chips, egg and chips, steak and chips and, 'Spanish' omelette and chips, which was basically an omelette with chips inside it. There were even bars advertising themselves as English pubs with fake wooden barrels and football on a tiny TV in the corner of the wall. The Spanish had pulled out all the stops to make us feel like we were at home. Such pubs were typically frequented by greasy red Englishmen, beaten by the unfamiliar scorching Spanish sun, seeking solace in a nice refreshing pint in a glass with a handle while they sweated profusely and looked like they were about to melt over the table. Young, shirtless men in Union Jack shorts and sometimes knotted Union Jack head hankies also frequented these places as they lapped up 'hair of the dog' after a busy night of heavy drinking and making brave and lewd passes at girls.

Women and children frequented the wide golden beaches. The women didn't look much better than the husbands they had left in the pubs. There were tits literally everywhere, spilling out on the beaches, regardless of age. You just didn't know where to look. I never knew women's breasts came in so many shapes, sizes and lengths until I went on my first holiday abroad; Tony's catalogue lingerie memories had been ruined. On our first day Tony and I had a ride on a banana boat with some other kids our age and when we got back to the beach we found Grandad Jimmy had managed to seek out the only German couple on the beach and was deep in conversation with them in their native language. I was surprised at this as he always swore if he ever met a German he would hang, draw and quarter them on the spot. Nanny Pearl said this was all a load of hot air as Grandad was about as scary as a Care Bear and besides, from what she could gather, they had been talking about Eurovision.

It didn't take long for Tony and me to meet hordes of other kids in the same way we had done when we were younger. The difference was that now we were older, more daring and had the freedom to make the entire town our own, our adventures were taking on a different theme. Whereas a few years ago we would have all had a day trip to the edge of a campsite to look at dead sheep in a stream, and ask kids from different regions what they were learning about in school, now our conversations went something like this:

'See that fit Geordie lad over there, right, he got drunk and shagged three girls last night. He'll do anything for a bottle of San Miguel, you don't even have to talk to him.'

And:

'There's a shop by our apartment that serves anyone booze as long as you're over twelve.'

And:

'Do you like my rings?' (Brandishes two hands weighed down with masses of sovereigns and huge gemstones.) 'They're real Spanish gold. Cost me nothing, you can rob anything from the market, as long as you buy some fruit off them.'

The thing was, none of this was Brian King style teenage bragging like it would have been at home. It was all true. For any teenager who experienced a summer holiday in Spain in the late 1980s, it was like a world where our parents, teachers and other adults seemed to have evaporated. While our parents enjoyed jugs of sangria and Camel cigarettes on balconies and terraces, all their teenage sons and daughters were running wild and having the most amazing time. The shops and markets were bursting with ceramics and leather, ceramic goods for the grown-ups and novelty gifts for us. Highly prized were the large range of weapons that could be bought or simply stolen to take home hidden in our suitcases. Tony and I were soon proud owners of a kosh, a knuckleduster, a flick knife and a set of throwing knives in various sizes which we would proudly show our friends when we returned home. There were also rude souvenirs such as Spanish porn playing cards and rubber pen toppers in the shape of religious figures that when you squeezed them produced a pair of rubber tits or a giant willy. Rude cartoon postcards that Benny Hill would have been proud of were snapped up from metal stands and sent enthusiastically to our friends back home with our adventures condensed and bragged into a few sentences. 'Hope you are well…Getting really drunk every night! It's ace here, got off with loads of people. Will bring back weapons, love Mel and Tony…xx'

What I liked the most was the bustling market and its large array of the fabled Spanish gold jewellery I had heard about. I had no jewellery of my own but longed for some like the gemstone rings my mother had. At first, I did buy myself a lovely gold ring with blue stones, which cost me my entire holiday money and a loan from Grandad Jimmy. With my Catholic school background, I would not have dared behave so terribly as to steal. However, after a few days swimming with it on it turned my finger green and the gold colour came off revealing a plastic band. I was fuming. I'd been well and truly ripped off, so after that I just did what everyone else was doing and before long I too was brandishing an elaborate ring on every finger. Tony had so many sovereigns and gold chains he looked like a skinny, white Mr T from *The A-Team*.

Every day we played about on the beach with groups of other teenagers. It was all tremendously friendly and no one had arguments or fights as there was no time to get bored. We took to the sea in pedalos, we climbed huge rocks and jumped off the top, and with the permanent rotation of teenagers there was someone new to fancy every day. Everyone was better-looking and funnier than our school friends back home – even I seemed to be better-looking and more confident, and boys were actually starting to pay me compliments for the first time in my life. Maybe I wasn't so awkward and weird looking after all.

After a very brief dinner (always something with chips) at a local taverna with our parents and grandparents it was time for the evening shenanigans, which would inevitably involve large amounts of San Miguel. It was true that anyone over twelve could get served, not just at some dodgy backstreet shop but in any bar in the Costa Brava. We made the absolute most of it. Everyone got drunk every night and we played spin the bottle and rolled around on the beach. Neither Tony or I wanted to go home.

By the second week our parents were ready to return home. Our dad's hair had turned purple as a result of him swimming in the pool (chlorine and cheap hair dye doesn't mix too well) and as there was no hair dye to be found in the shops, he had taken to pretending to have broken his toe and was spending as much time as possible in the apartment limping when he saw us. He refused to wear a hat or cap like a lot of the other men so Mom enjoyed a lot of peaceful reading on the beach while being brought cold drinks by taverna waiters. In the evenings she and our grandparents enjoyed the local entertainment planned especially for British tourists, over a few jugs of sangria. There was a hypnotist who made an example of Bill from Yorkshire, making him dance like a fairy in front of an hysterical crowd, and lots of team games where Brits would compete against each other to locate objects that the DJ would randomly shout out.

'Find me two bras!' he would shout into his microphone and the crowd would screech with laughter as drunken middle-aged people would rush about like headless chickens looking for the items. A few particularly competitive women would whip theirs off before the other contestants could rush back, brandishing them like victory flags.

'Find me a lemon attached to a branch!'

Off the contestants would go again, towards the nearest lemon tree which had been deliberately chosen as all the lemons were just slightly out of reach. It was quite a sight to see some overweight people jumping, with breathless, determined faces under those trees, while everyone laughed at them, until someone realised they needed a bunk-up.

Adults, it seemed, had also let themselves go on holiday, so they were less inclined to give us moral lectures. Grandad Jimmy sat with his new German friend, Harald, and they reminisced about how much had changed since the end of the war. No one knew how to behave any more, and no one seemed to care. Winston Churchill would be turning in his grave.

We were sad when it was time to go home and we desperately hoped that we could come back the next year. My parents and grandparents proudly packed their souvenir plates, painted maracas, and bullfighting snow globes ready to take pride of place on their G Plan units and Tony and I packed our cases, carefully concealing weapons, rude artefacts and stolen Spanish gold. We vowed never to go on holiday in the UK ever again!

What Teenagers Did Before Technology and Social Media

Most of the girls at my much-hated all-girls' comprehensive were incredibly intimidating, it was like finding yourself in some kind of cross between a hen do and a battlefield. They seemed so loud, so coarse and so white. A sea of pasty legs, bad perms, and scowling expressions.

In order to be popular at a large comprehensive girls' school you needed to know about fashion, pop music, smoking, recreational drug use, and be on first-name terms with the best-looking boys from the boys' school round the corner. For extra popularity points you needed to have won at least one fight in public against another girl who no one really liked, know how to shoplift without being caught, and have parents who probably didn't give a damn if you turned up at school looking like you were on the game. I didn't stand a chance in the popularity stakes. After a promising start of getting into The Dome nightclub at thirteen, which had meant that I'd got to know a few girls outside the school walls well enough to call them my friends, I was now under the watchful eye of my parents in case I did anything like that again. Strict curfews were imposed at weekends and during school holidays as my dad fretted over the possibility of any woe that could befall me.

Tony, being a boy, was allowed way more freedom as he was usually playing football, which was an actual social activity. At least, that's how it was explained to me when I protested. My dad felt that girls who 'walked the streets' and 'hung about in parks' and in groups of other girls were 'asking for trouble', in other words, were walking advertisements for underage sex and illegitimate babies.

After being inspired by a TV documentary I had seen called *Bombin,'* which was about the graffiti subculture, I retaliated by climbing out of the window at night to 'tag' my local area. I quickly met other kids doing the same and we would enjoy walking down the railway line to the city centre armed with cans of silver aluminium wheel paint (purchased from a local car paint shop every week after school, no questions asked). I was no Banksy, far from it, but it was very enjoyable and made a change from the home economics and needlework classes that were supposed to satisfy our creative urges at school. We would spray our tags everywhere from billboards, to bridges, to the sides of factories, before heading home at dawn just in time to scrub the paint off our hands and get ready for school. This went on for a few years until the local police decided to visit the boys' school to look at textbooks in order to identify the worst culprits. A few of the boys got caught out and the night-time hobby more or less stopped. The police never visited my school. They had missed a trick there. No one for one moment thought that one of the girls school's 'ladies' could ever be responsible for graffiti. Being female had some advantages because you were often underestimated.

A large part of my social life as a teenager in the late 1980s consisted of hanging about in parks in intimidating groups, that always seemed to include one or two teenage girls for whom the point of the English language was lost. Every time they opened their mouths all that came out was a deafening shriek or an over-the-top continuous laugh about nothing in particular. By the time they hit their teens this was Leese and Caz. They seemed to be permanently camped out in a park, or a shop doorway or even a wall, whichever was the chosen hang-out area of the month, probably because their parents could not bear to have them in the house. Being out in public with them was like babysitting feral toddlers.

Everywhere we tried to go with these two we were accompanied by this high-pitched wail and random laughter. It felt like you were witnessing comedy stand-up where most people had missed the punchline but no one dared admit it for fear of looking stupid. Anything anyone seemed to innocently say they managed to turn into some crude sexual innuendo for their own amusement. They would then shriek and squeal and double up with laughter at their jokes as if they were the funniest things ever.

Tony's social group was not much better. Teenage males also hung out in packs but instead of wailing banshees in their midst they had other phenomena, unique to their gender, and probably equally irritating, The first common member of the teenage boy species was the trainee alcoholic. This type of lad was usually around thirteen years old and identifiable by his hang-dog expression, slouchy zombie walk (usually trailing a beer mat swiped off a bar in the back pocket of his jeans as a symbol of recklessness) and a half-empty bottle of vodka poking out of his coat pocket. As an adult, anyone fitting this description is usually shunned by society, but according to teenage rules, which were contrary to those of intelligent adults, anyone fitting this description was immediately elevated to the status of a god. If he dared to push the boundaries to experimental drug use then he was so cool that any boy would be honoured to receive a grunt of recognition from him as he shuffled past on his way to the nearest pub (where of course he was always served and rumour had it he was shagging one of the barmaids) and any girl should be honoured to be chatted up by such a specimen (if they could actually understand any of the sentences he was trying to string together).

The other cool males in the gang were those who broke the law on a regular basis, with shoplifting, criminal damage and joyriding being top of the cool scale. Tony and his friend Brian King looked up to both these types and thought that they were the epitome of masculinity. I thought I might have to permanently disown my brother until I remembered that the extent of his and his friends' criminal career (in the UK anyway), was going to be tagging their pencil cases in permanent marker.

Brian King, who was at secondary school with Tony, was mates with all the cool kids and allegedly spent his weekends hot-wiring cars, picking up birds who were dead ringers for Page 3 girls and drinking so much vodka that Smirnoff had written to him personally and asked him to feature in their advertising campaigns (which would only be shown in Scotland due to 'lightweight' advertising rules). Brian King, did nothing of the sort. The closest he got to partially clothed ladies was enthusiastically searching the bushes in Rowheath Park for discarded jazz mags with Tony. Occasionally they struck gold and would spend the rest of the weekend in their bedrooms trying to figure out what bits went best where.

It was kids like the crude squawking girls, the trainee alcoholic and the aspiring criminal that were responsible for all the Neighbourhood Watch stickers in windows in Bournville.

I couldn't stand them. They were an embarrassment but it was like none of the others appeared to notice. It was their loudness and failure to adhere to rules that made them popular.

Having been brought up to believe that hard work and good manners would usually get you what you wanted, smoking and swearing were pastimes of the devil and it was only old men who bought Page 3 calendars, I was massively underprepared for teenage life at a comprehensive school. In short, I was destined to be a nerd.

In the 80s our social life had to be organised in advance. Because mobile phones had not been invented, and without the powers of telepathy at our disposal, a designated meeting spot was earmarked for those who were not grounded and could persuade their parents to let them out for a few hours. In summer this was generally a wall in the local park. Whatever time of an evening or weekend you wandered down to the wall outside the cricket pavilion, there were at least a couple, and sometimes a whole herd, of squawking adolescents lolling about, dreaming of house parties and how to afford the latest pop music cassette. In winter our meeting place was the recessed entrance of the Levines furniture shop in Cotteridge, where we shivered and shared damp cigarettes that we had pestered passers-by to donate to us. It was cold and mostly boring but we were there to show solidarity with our school-mates and if we didn't show up we might miss something important: a secret plan, some idle gossip or somebody falling over.

If we were really lucky we could bypass some of the compul-sory attendance in person and use the landline at home. We listed our friends' phone numbers in diaries and alphabetic phone books, alongside doodled hearts and arrows with the names of people we fancied intertwined with ours, or if you were a boy like Tony, the doodles were names of the football team you supported alongside sketches of numerous penises in permanent states of arousal.

The phone was always fastened securely onto a wall or table in the most public place in the house so that your parents, could hear everything you said, as well as time your conversation. Our's was in the hallway on its own special table with its own special seat from which everything you said reverberated around the house.

This meant that talking in whispers, slang or personalised code was necessary, to prevent nosey parents finding out your personal business. Sometimes they would stand there and point at their watch or sometimes they would just stand there and eyeball you and refuse to budge until you were forced to hang up. This would be followed by 'reasoning' arguments from your parents around things such as needing to keep the landline free and how we couldn't have anything more to say to our friends after being at school with them all day, and finally how much it was costing every minute we used the damn thing. Many teenagers would come home one day to find the phone sporting a giant lock to which only our parents held the key. The phone lock became the ultimate 80s symbol of frustration for teenagers.

So, there was nothing for it but to either make a plan at school to meet at the designated area, or if we wanted to be spontaneous we could walk to our friends' houses, ring the bell and ask if they were in.

Another thing that my friends and I liked to do was go shopping to Birmingham city centre. Spending Saturdays in the city centre shops, in between Saturday jobs, was a must.

This was where we kept an eye on the latest fashions. We couldn't afford most of them but it was great fun trying things on just to see what we would look like, emulating the fashion features we had gazed adoringly at in *Just Seventeen* magazine.

By the late 80s hip-hop culture was starting to influence teenage fashion so we adorned ourselves in baggy jeans, hooded tops, chunky fake gold jewellery and loosely laced trainers or boots. We walked in groups, hair gelled and moussed so much that our curls looked wet and our fringes were stiff and vertical. Some groups of girls had fringes so high and spiky they looked like small herds of dinosaurs as they stalked the aisles in Boots, loudly discussing the merits of wash-in hair tints and coloured mousse. The former was the definite winner as the dye from the mousse used to run down your neck and clothes if you got caught in the rain.

Fashion was becoming dominated by high street giants and no trip to town was complete without a look around Miss Selfridge, Top Shop and Hennes where we would each gather armfuls of brightly coloured tops and rush off to the changing rooms. Once there we were transformed into pop stars as we twisted and shrieked like birds of paradise showering each other with compliments or laughing hysterically at our chosen attire. After a lengthy period of time we would sheepishly emerge to hand our armfuls of rejected clothing to the changing room assistant without making eye contact and muttering something about how they 'didn't fit' so that our poverty would not be rumbled. We would then move onto the next shop where the whole changing room process would start again. When a beautiful new wedding shop appeared in one of the arcades, we simply had to try it out. We came up with a not-very-convincing plan that Jenny, being the tallest of us all, was the bride-to-be. A few hours later we were chased out and banished by a very angry store owner, who returned to find most of her wedding and bridesmaid dresses lying in an explosion across the changing room floor, and one nervous shop assistant standing in a corner.

Lunch was usually a brief stop at McDonald's where at least our pocket money always stretched to a Big Mac and fries before we were off again. We absolutely had to mentally furnish our future homes with a visit to The Reject Shop. Then it was off to The Body Shop to inhale and dab on an array of beautiful samples. The perfume rack with its glass droppers beckoned us to drop scents with names like 'Dewberry' and 'Visionary' on our wrists, the tiny sample bottles and bath beads allowed us to inhale the delights of banana, strawberry and jojoba. One small bottle was within our price range so we rarely left there empty-handed.

There was a new indoor shopping centre that was an exciting vision of the future called the The Pavilions. By the late 1980s these micro-copies of American malls had started to pop up in every city. Ours was four storeys high with a glass lift in the centre. The lift was as fascinating as the shops themselves. Like the great glass elevator from *Charlie and the Chocolate Factory*, up you would go, leaving the lower floor shoppers behind until they looked like a swarm of ants below your feet and you could survey your empire of purchasing possibilities from up high. The lift never crashed through the roof like it did in the book; instead it went to the food court, an entire floor of culinary opportunities from around the world. You could grab your food and go. We would stroll around, carefully considering the many kiosks offering Chinese, Indian, pizza, baked potatoes as well as well as other outlets including a French deli before settling for our usual Coke or frothy milkshakes in tall glasses.

Between the shops and the train station was an area known as 'the ramp' which was where the worst of Birmingham's teenage lowlifes would lie in wait to 'tax' unsuspecting shoppers of their gold jewellery. I remember seeing them and feeling intimidated but of course they never bothered us – after all a teenage girl with £1.50 in her pocket, and a small bottle of Body Shop Banana Conditioner was hardly going to be a worthwhile mugging opportunity.

We would then get the train back to Cotteridge where half of us ('the sensible, boring ones') would walk home and try to persuade our parents to unlock the landline while the other half ('he screechy, popular ones') would get off the bus and immediately latch onto whichever teenage boy happened to be in the vicinity at the time and not let him out of their clutches until he agreed to snog one of them or give them some fags. One time they were delighted to spot Vinny Thompson by the bus stop. Vinny, who by now had become our own personal 'Zammo' from *Grange Hill,* had spent the entire day eating magic mushrooms 'for a laugh' and had been trying to walk into a closed shop doorway since lunchtime, attempting to reach the magic kingdom he knew was within. He never got there. His mother kept him off school for weeks after that due to his fears of persecution.

Champagne Charlies and The 'Offy'

My first job was working in Champagne Charlie's kebab and chip shop when I was thirteen. I wanted to work there because there was a girl in my class, Donna, who had a job working on the till. She was paid an impossibly huge amount of money for working there after school, rumoured to be thirty pounds a week, which was generally unattainable for a teenager. After so many wishful thinking shopping trips to The Pavilions I thought I would like some of that, so one day I decided to have a chat with Natalia, the fierce Greek lady who owned it, and volunteer my services.

To my absolute surprise, and despite having zero work experience, I was hired on the spot and promised the princely sum of £25.00 a week for three days after school and Saturday mornings. I was absolutely delighted, until I turned up for my first shift and found that I was relegated to the freezing back room and shown all the huge sacks of potatoes that I had to transform into chips for the customers: five sacks per shift!

First, I had to tip them into a noisy whirring machine that stripped them of their muddy coats and plonked them into a vat of cold water. Then I had to scoop the damn things out, one at a time, examine them for the scabby pieces the machine had

145

missed, of which there were plenty, and remove them manually with a knife before throwing them in a plastic bin full of yet more cold water. They would stay here until Natalia's grown-up son would shuffle in, brandishing some sort of metal potato torture rack, then plunge his hairy hands into the water and select his victims. Then they were ready to fry up for the throng of customers who were always forming a line in the shop for my cheery outgoing classmate to serve.

By the end of my second week, by which time I had cuts and chilblains on my hands and would finish my shift unable to feel my own feet for the biting cold of the back room, I decided to chance it and asked Natalia if there was any chance of a promotion to work on the till one day.

She looked up fiercely from where she had been shaking the sacks of discarded potato peelings as though she was panning for gold before half-laughing and half-shouting back at me.

'I would never put you on the till because of your face!'

That was harsh. I was only good enough to be hidden away like a hunchback in the back room. Right, I didn't care if the money meant I could plunder The Body Shop every weekend. The shame wasn't worth it. I would look for another job, even if the pay was 'crap' like Tony's £5 *Birmingham Chronicle* paper round. He dumped them at the back of the garages anyway and no one missed them. I reckoned that the next time we had heavy rainfall, the residents of Bournville would have their own papier-mâché sea with the amount of papers he dumped every week.

As I looked in the mirror that night in my room I wondered what was wrong with me. I figured that maybe Natalia had a bit of a point. Maybe it was the band of chemically triggered acne that framed my hairline, but then again, most girls in the 80s had the same problem. It was a trade-off for the daily training of fringes into vertical slopes on top of our heads. Hairspray and a blast of the hairdryer set the look each morning. The halo of hairline acne was thought to be a small price to pay for fashion, but if it was ruining my chances of promotion then maybe I should rein it in.

The final straw for me at Champagne Charlie's was when we had heavy snow one week and when I went to collect my wage envelope Natalia told me she had docked my pay by twenty pounds. Apparently the snow had affected her sales. I couldn't believe the cheek of it! I was actually speechless. Instead of challenging her (as I fantasised about later), I meekly accepted the slavery fee and trudged sadly home; no Saturday shopping jaunt for me that weekend.

I was due back in on Monday evening, but decided I couldn't trust Natalia again. However, I felt a bit guilty for leaving her and her potatoes in the lurch so I asked screeching big mouth Caz to go in my place. She gratefully accepted the opportunity. Within a week she was serving customers at the till.

Most of my friends were working after school or at weekends by this time. With it being the 80s, when no one really abided by child labour laws or reasonable pay, it was easy to get part-time work. Most of the work was blatant exploitation by greedy small-time employers. Hilary rang the necks of turkeys at a poultry farm for twenty pence a kill, and chased the headless bodies if they were deluded enough to think they could get away. Kelly stuffed sausage skin with all manner of pig remains that she had ground up herself, and my next job was at an 'offy' which sold alcohol, cigarettes, and magazines to the people of Cotteridge.

My friends, and friends of their friends, thought that it was the best job in the world. I wasn't old enough to buy most of the things in the shop, but I could sell them.

The store owner spent the first day I was there telling every local teenager to 'clear off'. The way they were queueing up outside that shop when I was the only one on the till, you would have thought that Bros was putting in a personal appearance. I stayed there for a few years and quite enjoyed it, apart from the occasional rudeness of adult customers who were impatient for their Benson & Hedges. It seemed that most working-class adults smoked back then, so most of their teenage children followed suit. It was too easy to stand outside an offy or newsagent and find a sympathetic adult to buy cigarettes for kids.

We had all been influenced in the early part of the decade by Superman's crusade against Nick O' Teen, the pro-smoking cartoon baddie who recruited kids to smoke, and we were rewarded with posters for our abstinence. However those campaigns were for primary school children and by the time we were at secondary school there was nothing to stop us. Teachers could smoke in staff rooms, grown ups could smoke in offices and many of the trendy black and white photos that adorned our bedroom walls featured cool models and Hollywood greats, fag dangling casually from their mouths. Smoking was risqué and cool.

My favourite thing about working at the offy was not the vast quantities of fags and booze on offer, but the magazines. Every time I had a lunch break I could take my pick from anything on the shelf as long as I put it back afterwards.

I devoured the pop song lyrics in *Smash Hits*, which were never ever what you had thought they were before you read them. Grandad Jimmy, who always complained loudly, when

Tony and I watched *Top of the Pops*, that it wasn't real music and you couldn't make out what they were singing about, was right after all. Paul Young had *not* sung about someone taking a piece of meat with them every time they went away, Brian Adams did *not* have his first real sex dream in the summer of '69 and Robert Palmer sang about someone being addicted to love, not a 'dick' with a glove! Who would have guessed before those magazines started printing song lyrics?

Using this wealth of magazines, I educated myself about how to catch and keep a boyfriend, I had more sex information than I ever would have had at school, I learned how to dress like an independent successful woman (shoulder pads and coloured eyeshadow), and thanks the huge variety of car magazines, learned how to pimp a Mini Cooper with so many accessories that it would look like a small tank, with an exhaust so huge you could put an extra passenger in it.

Parties and Bad Hair

I don't know how the park parties began. All I remember was that during the long, hot six-week summer holidays of 1989 my friend Jenny and her sixth-form lover stepped up their relationship by getting serious; in other words, he bought her an eternity ring. Jenny was good as married! This only meant one thing. We knew someone who could buy us alcohol. Every Saturday we used to persuade that boy to meet us outside the offy where we would give him all our hard-earned slave wages and pocket money and in return he would go shopping for us.

Out he would come, laden with crates of Diamond White, Thunderbird and Mad Dog 20/20 and we would run gleefully to our local park to drink it and gain confidence, wit and humour that we never knew we were capable of possessing. News travelled fast and within a few Saturdays the sixth-former was buying enough alcohol to supply D-Day celebrations in London. There were so many bags and crates that he had to make several trips back and forth to the offy just to carry them out. If by that stage he wanted to get out of the arrangement there was just no way he could have done so. The army that had formed from the local secondary schools would have chased him out of Birmingham in anger and Carly Trueman would have sat on his head to hasten his demise.

Diamond White and Thunderbird tasted foul, they were nothing like the gentle fruity tones of our parents' Blue Nun or Liebfraumilch but they got you drunk quickly and it was like being transported into another universe. Our local park was spacious enough that we could all hide ourselves and our activities away from the small kids in the play areas and the dog walkers on the perimeter paths. There were huge vacant fields, small valleys and woods where we could hold our own parties without arousing suspicion or creating a noisy nuisance and we absolutely made the most of it.

Once the revolting magical brew had taken hold of our bodies and minds we had the most interesting stories and jokes to tell; the plainest people suddenly developed attractive qualities and if you had a secret crush on anyone, now was the time to reveal it and the chances were your crush would be more than happy to kiss you for the flattery. If anyone latched onto you and tried to pester you inappropriately, you simply gave him a shove and watched him roll away down the grass bank, a most hilarious sight and without repercussions as you knew that they would forget about it in a few minutes and find someone else to bother. Yes, park parties quickly became the highlight of the summer.

That was until the novelty of waking up freezing cold on dew-covered grass, with your grass-stained shell suit sticking to your skin, wore off. We would traipse home, dodging the puke puddles as we went, only to get our parents up with a sorry tale about the tent falling down (we had allegedly been camping in a friend's garden).

By the winter of that year the park party craze had died out and we tried our luck with the clubs again, even though by the late 80s they were starting to wize up and scrutinise our fake NUS cards. We had to wait for the occasional event of someone's parents being daft enough to go away for the weekend leaving their teenage child alone in the house. This very rare occasion was always taken advantage of. Outfits would be planned, hair would be styled and excuses for staying out for the night would be conspired. For me it was always homework. Homework on a Saturday night, a special school project that was being done in conjunction with a female friend. In reality, the special school project would consist of us attempting to do home perms and make-up in order for us to look as attractive as possible; choosing between the shell suit or the baggy blue jeans or the multi-coloured jester trousers.

We would sit in our bedrooms and attempt a home perm or try to curl our hair with bendy pink rollers. They rarely worked and we never ended up looking like the girl on the box. Usually only part of the perm would take so you would be left with a curly fringe and the rest of your hair dead straight. A good perm was the holy grail for girls – and boys.

The home hair colouring attempts were no better. One of the 'must have' products of the 80s was Sun In spray. This was basically bleach in a bottle masquerading as some sort of miracle that would transform your boring mousy (or even dark) locks into sun-kissed Californian blonde. All you had to do was spray your hair enthusiastically, blast with a hairdryer and hey presto – you had a beautiful new shade of …erm …ginger, …with dark patches where you had missed bits. If you then attempted it enough times your hair might eventually become blonde, but it would also snap off when you brushed it, so you ended up looking more Worzel Gummidge than Christie Brinkley.

Sensible people, on the advice of proper hairdressers, went blonde gradually by having highlights. This involved stretching a plastic half-colander, half-helmet over your head and then using a kind of torture hook instrument to ram through the holes and pull out strands of hair all over your head until you eventually looked like you could have starred in a horror film. I used to fear going to the hairdresser's to have this done in case they put me in a chair in front of the window for anyone walking past to see and recoil in horror at my bald plastic scalp with a few mad tendrils escaping from it. The tendrils would then be painted with stinky blue ointment, you would be left under a hot dryer for a while and then the cap would be removed, which involved it being ripped painfully off your head to reveal your original locks now 'enhanced' with stripes of blonde. It probably looked OK if you had been a natural blonde to start with, but for anyone with darker hair you just looked like a half-human half-zebra experiment. To sum it up, hairstyles in the 1980s were probably the worst hairstyles in the history of the world, and these bad hairstyles were what we spent many hours of our lives trying to re-create in order to make ourselves more attractive, especially for up and coming parties.

Teenage house parties of the 80s resembled Dante's *Inferno* crossed with a Roman orgy mixed with an explosion at an off-licence. I am a mother of teenagers now and they think their parties are pretty wild. Well, I can tell you that teenage parties today are like going to church compared to what ours were like.

There were no invitations and no planning. All you had to do was utter the words, 'house party', at any time and in any location and as if by magic every teenager within a ten-mile radius would hear the magical words whispered on the wind and they would use their psychic powers to deduce the date, the address and the fact that there would be no adults present.

The day would come and all manner of excuses would be doled out to parents: homework project, camping in a friend's garden, invited to a sleepover. We had to be prepared to stay out all night. There would always be some boy whose voice had broken early and quite dramatically who would be appointed someone's dad for convincing phone calls.

He would stand in the phonebox while an orderly queue would form outside with ten-pence pieces, and home phone numbers written on scraps of paper. His job was to telephone parents and ask if a certain child was allowed to stay the night with his teenage son. This usually worked a treat, although some parents were sharper than others and then the cover was blown. The deep-voiced boy also tried his best to impersonate a woman but the attempt was doomed from the start because he sounded like a boy with a deep voice doing a very bad impersonation of a high-pitched woman who had just stubbed her toe. The teenage chancer would then be immediately rumbled and had to go straight home to be grounded.

Buying alcohol was easy. As we were well aware by now, once dolled up a girl could often get served in a shop by the age of thirteen, no questions asked. If this attempt did fail then you just followed a sixth-former around and pestered him until he agreed to buy your cheap cider for you.

Finding the party was easy as you could hear the commotion from several streets away and you would follow the throng of kids making their way towards it, openly carrying their illegally purchased alcohol. Outside the house in question there would be crowds of gatecrashers trying to force their way in, having

154

an argument with someone at the door who was trying to tell them the place was full, couples rolling around on the front lawn, several people crying hysterically and some boy having an imaginary shouting match with no one in particular and threatening to rip off someone's head, while all around him his friends would be going, 'Ssh, be quiet or the neighbours might guess there's a party!'

Once you had squeezed your way inside, the entire house and every room would be packed shoulder to shoulder with teenagers. If you needed the bathroom you had to start making the journey about an hour before you actually felt the need. Sometimes there would be music coming from a wannabe DJ in the kitchen, but more often than not there was no music, the ghetto blaster having been drowned out by the chatter, laughter and screaming of the mob.

All you did when you were there was attempt to squeeze your way past other guests and look for someone of the opposite sex who looked interesting enough to talk to. Once you found one it was usually the case that conversation was impossible due to the background noise, and the fact that the object of your attention was probably so drunk that no intelligible words would come out of them. So you just sat or stood next to them, swigging from whatever disgusting brew you had with you and trying to find out their name and where they hung out, hoping they didn't vomit at your feet.

The police would inevitably roll up around half-time in their riot vans. To the shout of 'pigs!' everyone who could still walk would escape out the back of the house, over neighbours' fences if necessary, to evade being gathered up and thrown into the back of those vans. Those who could fake sobriety would walk back to their homes and report that the 'school project' had gone well.

Everyone Wants to be a Supermodel

One day, Leese, Caz and Carly Trueman decided that they wanted to become fashion models. The birth of 'the super-model' in the late 80s, and the fortune and fame that level of modelling could bring, made it the fantasy career of many teenage girls. You could forget having a brown folder with 'Record of Achievement' on the front, which we were told by our teachers was all we needed for future career success. If you could make it as a model you were a guaranteed millionaire and you could throw that damn folder on the fire.

To supply the thirst of the aspiring model, many new modelling agencies sprung up, which promised to help you build a portfolio – an essential step if you wanted to make it big in the modelling world. Then they would introduce you to their contacts so you could be the next Yasmin Le Bon. All you had to do was give them your parents' life savings first!

Carly Trueman had met a 'model scout' in a pub who assured her that she had what it took and had given her an invitation to a 'How to be a Model' presentation his agency was giving in a hotel in Birmingham city centre. Naturally all of my friends wanted to go. The 80s was the decade of easy fame and aspirational wages and everyone wanted some. There was no way anyone was missing out on the chance to be a model.

My mom said it was a con. My Grandad Jimmy exclaimed, 'Carly Trueman! A model? What for? Save the Whale?' before being swatted with a newspaper by Nanny Pearl and told not to insult a lady's waistline. I had read so many articles in my off-licence magazines about how no reputable modelling agency would ever ask you to pay them money in advance, so I was highly suspicious. I knew it reeked of a scam but I was curious. I mean it was only a talk after all and if anyone tried to get money out of me or any of my friends they were targeting the wrong people. Our disposable income was a tenner a week if we were lucky.

Tony took the piss out of me and my friends all week leading up to the talk. At the time the TV show *Bread* was very popular and one of the main female characters, Aveline, was an aspiring, although deluded, 'model'. Tony and Brian King donned my mom's old high heels and, fur coats and stomped up and down the hall like bad transvestites shouting in a Scouse accent. 'Terrar Ma, I'm going modellin',' every time any of my friends came round. They really were embarrassing and I wished I had never mentioned it.

On the day of the talk we met at Cotteridge train station and there was a buzz of excitement and bragging in the air.

'He reckoned that you can make the front cover of *Vogue* in twelve months,' said Carly smugly sucking in her midriff. Her proud and rounded mother had come along for the event, but I reckoned she fancied her chances too as she was dressed almost identically to her daughter. They had chosen to wear trendy, but hideous, neon orange skin-tight dresses in a kind of crinkly fabric and they had their permed hair in what were known as 'pineapples', which resembled palm trees growing out of the top of their heads. In addition to this, Carly had been on the SlimFast shakes and reckoned she'd lost a whole six pounds in a week, although her mother had told her not to lose any more in case she lost her 'curves' and ended up like one of those anorexics. There was little chance of that. They were both so round they looked like rejects from the space hopper factory.

Next to them were Leese and Caz who, to be fair, if it wasn't for the chain-smoking and persistent screeching were naturally pretty girls, Donna, who worked at Champagne Charlie's and didn't care for a modelling career, but didn't want to miss anything, and Jenny, who was going out with the sixth-former and had nothing better to do that day as he was on his enforced off licence tour. Finally, there was me, in a white shell suit, sheepish, but secretly hoping for a miracle that would transport me away from embarrassing brothers and their stupid friends, foul-mouthed older girls who actually wanted to spend more time with my embarrassing brother, and teachers that behaved like Roald Dahl villains.

The talk itself was at one of the posh hotels in the city centre and was led by a oily-haired man in a suit. So far so good. There were about a hundred teenage girls there all listening keenly, dressed in their finest outfits and flicking their hair. None of them stood out as being overly attractive, or over the age of fourteen, and I got the impression that Carly's model scout had been handing out cards to any teenage females he could find just to get bums on seats.

The talk covered what to expect if you became a model, which was sound advice according to what I had read in magazines: lots of castings, travelling to castings, rejections, the need to keep a normal day job, and the need to get something called an 'Equity card' if you wanted to appear on television. Finally, there was a question and answer session with attendees asking such gems such as:

'Would you recommend eating a tapeworm to help keep slim and get more work?'

'I have bought a cell phone so I'm contactable all the time' (Produces plastic breeze block from handbag.) 'What time should I expect phone calls?'

'I don't think I need an Equity card because I was on *The Pink Windmill* once and Rod Hull and Emu thought I was a natural.'

The man leading the talk then said he was going to go round the room and if he put his hand on top of your head this meant he thought you were in with a chance and you could go to the stage and have some 'test shots' taken. If he passed you by then unfortunately you were not cut out for being a model and could go home. This was an awfully embarrassing situation to be in. Rejected publicly for being as ugly as sin. There was no way I wanted this so I quickly stood up, excused myself and went out through the glass doors at the back of the hall. I stood awkwardly in the corridor waiting for my friends and peeking curiously through the glass door to see what the next group of supermodels looked like.

The oily-haired one walked along the rows of chairs and patted a few heads like he was playing some boring kid's party game. There were sobs from some of the girls he missed out. There were shrieks of delight from those who were chosen, along with matching squeals of excitement and pride from their mothers. Then they would jump up and run full throttle at the stage. It was like watching a kids' version of *The Price is Right*. Then I suddenly noticed that he was only choosing the girls who very obviously had their parents with them. He didn't seem to be looking at the girls before he chose them but he was definitely looking very carefully at their parents.

My suspicions were confirmed when he picked out Carly Trueman. These were the days before anyone really used plus-size models but even if he had been looking for one, Carly was only 4ft 11, she had the walk of a charging rhino and a face suited only to radio – and, that was being generous. The whole model search was indeed a con. All they were interested in was extracting money from these girls' gullible parents.

I said hardly anything on the way home. It was easier not to. Besides, no one could get a word in edgeways between the excitable chatter of Carly and her mom about her glittering future. Paris, New York and Milan catwalks awaited her. According to Carly none of us had what it took, because I looked 'too foreign', Leese was 'too thin', Caz was 'too girl next door', Jenny was 'too shy' and Donna 'would have got in but probably smelled a bit like a kebab'. Her mother just sat there beaming at Carly like she was some sort of religious icon. I think we were all too dumbstruck by how much the promise of wealth could change an individual in an instant. Carly had always been arrogant and prone to random acts of selfishness but now all I could think about was the first time I met my witty primary school friend, Colleen Fahey, the one who had three older brothers. We had both been four years old and were listening to Brian King talking about how Father Christmas had to put a roof rack on his sleigh just for the extent of gifts his parents bought him. She quipped, 'If your head gets any bigger you are in danger of hitting the clouds and knocking over God!'

I wished I could think of something similarly smart to say to Carly but Leese beat me to it when she said, 'Well, at least you can buy your own hairspray now!'

For the next few months all we heard about (and giggled mercilessly about behind her back) was Carly Trueman's modelling career. The portfolio her mother faithfully paid the agency a small fortune to create consisted of just four cringe-worthy photos. These apparently demonstrated the flexibility of the model. One photo showed Carly pretending to be a secretary and looking gormless while holding a phone, another was a head and shoulders shot where she was draped in a feather boa, pearls and a satin scarf (so it looked like an evening gown). A third showed her climbing out of a pool in the Caribbean (except he pool was a background freeze and she was actually ascending a stepladder that had been plonked in a paddling pool) and last but not least a sultry-looking over-the-shoulder pose where she had the same expression as someone who had just been caught red-handed by the police.

It fizzled out as suddenly as it had begun after she came back from a very expensive weekend where she had been 'taught' how to walk the catwalk. A chance dinnertime conversation with some older girls at school revealed that there were loads of them who had exactly the same portfolio, had been made the same promises of fame and then, once their parents had handed over much of their life savings, their 'career' went eerily quiet, telephone messages were never returned and the agency manager was always 'away on business'. Carly went back to throwing her weight around (literally) and hundreds of other wannabe models up and down the country were taken in by the same con.

The Pursuit of Pleasure

I remember the arrival of our first Betamax video recorder. Our parents had been desperate for one for ages. Tony and I spent the first day continually pressing the fast forward and rewind buttons as it was so funny to make people speed walk. Grandad Jimmy and Nanny Pearl had welcomed a video recorder into their gold and brown house ages before us and had wasted no time investing in a special G-Plan bookcase and stacks of leather-look video cassette holders embossed with gold scrawl which everyone said looked just like Victorian novels. They quickly built up quite a library in their lounge.

The best thing about being the proud owners of a video recorder was that on Friday evenings our dad would take us to the local video shop and we could choose a film to watch for the weekend. The local video shop was an outing in itself. Every wall was completely covered in shelf upon shelf of video cassette boxes ready to tempt you into watching them with their eye-catching pictures. Each area of shelving would be clearly labelled with the film genres, usually with neon stars stuck to each area, with hastily scribbled wording in felt pen saying, 'horror', 'romance', 'drama', 'adults only', and, 'three for two special offer'.

You had to be quick off the mark on a Friday evening as all the new releases would get snapped up quickly. Often you had to book the most popular films weeks in advance to be able to rent them. In the absence of online film reviews you had to rely on word of mouth from your mates or on the information on the outside of the case in order to decide if it would be worth watching. Deciding what to watch involved examining many boxes and excitedly gathering handfuls of them, sometimes to be told, 'We're not watching that!' by an irritated parent who would tell you to put the '18'-rated one back. Once you and the rest of your family (or rather your dad) had agreed on which one to rent, you went excitedly to the counter where a member of staff would take the empty box and go and look out the back for your cassette. It would then be put in a plain box (the ones with the pictures were display only!) and off you would go with your exciting film, all yours for the weekend.

The arrival of MTV and the expansion of satellite television was also starting to open up many more exciting possibilities of things to watch. It gave us pop videos on tap which brought our idols closer to us and brought our bedroom posters to life. The availability of adult-only channels livened up a lot of teenage boys' (and probably their dads') evenings, even if they did have to block their doors and turn the sound down. By contrast women could go and see male strippers in their local pub, and groups like the Chippendales became popular with frustrated middle-aged housewives and single women who screamed hysterically with delight at the sight of an oiled-up bloke wearing a bow tie and a thong. Boundaries were starting to be pushed in every area of British culture and we couldn't get enough of it. Everywhere you went people were looking to have fun.

Each year in our community, traditional festivals and travelling fairs still took place as they had done for centuries. An adjoining village, had one each summer and it was looked forward to with great enthusiasm because of the social opportunities it would present. If you stayed there all day you would usually bump into everyone you had ever known; it was like your own personal version of *This is Your Life.*

There were all the traditional stalls that sold plants, home-made cakes and local crafts, along with a maypole display, a helter skelter, a coconut shy and a fortune teller in a tent who made up stories about your future for fifty pence a go. There was only ever one concession to modernity and that was a fairground ride that was about as 80s as you could get. We knew it as the 'Meteorite' and it looked like a hybrid of a wheel and a cage. For a small fee a group of people could stand in a circle inside it while it spun around and tilted vertically, the riders pinned to the sides by the centrifugal force. This was well before people really considered any kind of health and safety issues, and 'compensation culture' was unheard of. We found it hugely exciting as we spun around, feeling as though we could fall out at any moment. If you wanted to behave in an even more risqué manner and prove your bravado you could turn around and face the inner wall (this wasn't all that much fun since your face would be squashed to the point you felt you would stop breathing), or you could climb near the top so that when the ride started your head might be able to poke over the top. The ride owners didn't care about the risk of decapitation or asphyxiation, as long as we had paid the fifty pence for our go.

In the evenings, when the older generation and families had gone home with their lemon drizzle cakes and their aloe vera plants, the festival ground became a swarm of teenagers and young adults looking for coupling opportunities. The contents of parents' drinks cupboards and cheap supermarket lager would be sneaked in under denim jackets and down the legs of shell suits. These would be consumed under cover of darkness while we flirted and laughed and waited for the extravagant firework display that was always the climax of the evening's festivities.

There was a similar annual event on our village green known as the 'Mop'. This was a centuries-old travelling fair that had originally been for people to seek employment. By the 80s it was a funfair and an opportunity for the local crooks to pick pockets and 'tax' people of their jewellery. However, as the average teenager wore no valuable items it was generally safe to wander around and have a go on as many rides as our pocket money would allow. Once, Jenny and I went on a ride we called 'eggs in space'. It was like a rusty Ferris wheel with individual cages, just big enough for two people to sit in (think the London Eye if it had been manufactured by primitive man) and every now and again a Neanderthal would come along and spin you 360 degrees until you screamed. Anyway, while we were being spun round by someone with no teeth, the metal bolt fell out of the door and landed on Jenny's lap. We screamed some more and the Neanderthal, misinterpreting our terror as pleasure, began to grin widely and spun us some more. We had to hold the door shut for the rest of the ride. When we got off and handed in the bolt, someone just put it back in the door, gave it a good whack and carried on like nothing had happened!

The school disco was another annual event that we always looked forward to. It was always a sell-out as it was the only opportunity within school property where both the boys,' and girls' school could mingle. Outfit planning took weeks! Everyone looked so different out of uniform and my friends and I would have the opportunity to study the opposite sex at close range and not just in passing. There was no getting away. We could stare all we liked!

The freedom to dress up like the adults who went to clubs in the town, and to dance outside of the constraints of our bedrooms, was amazing. Helped along by semi-darkness and the confidence that unlimited gel and hairspray gave us, we were in our element. The dizzy excitement of being able to check out the opposite sex and for them to check us out in return was a novelty. At the end of the 'disco' the DJ would always play a slow romantic track and then, like an unspoken code, every boy had to locate a girl to dance with. If you were lucky, you got a decent-looking one. If you weren't so lucky you usually said yes to any boy that asked and were grateful that it was dark and you could look over his shoulder and smile (or snigger) at your friends while silently relishing the aroma of Insignia aftershave on his skin.

The school discos got banned after Vinny Thompson and his friends brought the skeleton down from the science labs to join in the dancing. Unfortunately, during a rather energetic version of Salt-N-Pepa's' 'Push It,' its neck snapped and its skull shot across the dance floor and wedged under some girls who were gyrating on stacked chairs. Their hysteria unleashed a riot which resulted in them being pelted with bones. I guess chivalry was truly in its death throes around then.

The summer of 1989 was one that I remember particularly fondly as it was a scorcher. On our way to the city it was so hot that it felt as though our shell suits were melting onto our bodies. Some of my female friends and I had taken to wearing bikinis and swimsuits as tops, like we were going to one of the raves that had started to gain popularity in the music scene. Tony and his friends wore bum bags and gun holsters over their rolled up shell suit bottoms and listened to N.W.A. singing about 'Fuck Tha Police'. Teenage boys fantasised about being gangsters, and being black and 'from the streets' became the epitome of cool.

We went to see the film *House Party'* at the Futurist cinema and a week later many of the boys had shaved their heads, with the exception of a square block on top. They were mostly white boys and looked more astro turf than cool but they swaggered around Cotteridge and Rowheath like they owned the place.

At school breaktimes we played rounders or football in the fields or lay about attempting to sunbathe and get a fashionable tan. Some of us were lucky enough to have sunbeds at home which were used with alarming regularity in order to look like we had just got back from a holiday in the 'Med'. Sometimes we clubbed together and rented sunbeds that hooked over our beds at home and lay under them after school, blissfully unaware of the dangers. Sun In spray, highlights and perms were applied and re-applied, by boys and girls alike. We wanted to look like we were from *Neighbours* or *Home and Away* or ready to be spotted by a music label at any moment. We had heard on the grapevine that you didn't even need to be able to sing to be a pop star, and judging by the amount of soap stars turning their hands to making records it seemed feasible enough and the possibility of instant fame and celebrity fuelled many daydreams.

Tony formed a boy band with Brian King and some other friends. They didn't get as far as actually singing anything but did get some promotional photos done of them all wearing jeans with boxers poking over the top while they all looked in different directions. They would pore over copies of car magazines and plan which huge kits and accessories they would get to put on their future cars. Some of the other local boys discovered that Metros, Maestros and Montego cars were easy to break into and 'hot-wire', which led to the regular weekend hobby of 'joyriding' in stolen cars. There was always someone showing off 'their' car with pride before word got out and they had to abandon it somewhere quiet. Very few joyriders were actually caught due to security cameras being so rare. Property crime flourished in the 80s for this reason the sense of entitlement was growing. If you couldn't afford something then you could always try to obtain it by other means.

My grandparents were baffled by it all. The concept of not saving up for things because you could get them on the never-never or by illegal means was all that was wrong with the younger generation, in their opinion. I had started coming home from trips to the town centre every Saturday armed with knock-off cassettes that some bloke was selling out of a suitcase for a fraction of the real price outside HMV. There would be friends of friends selling fake neon Joe Bloggs and Naf Naf t-shirts or Ray-Bans that we could actually afford and we willingly handed over five-pound notes to obtain them. Ethics didn't come into it; besides Del Boy Trotter from *Only Fools and Horses* was adored throughout the UK and he was doing exactly the same thing. We paraded our knocked off fashions though shopping centres and parks with pride. We were as loud and as bright as peacocks in mating season. We were the future and the future was bright; it was more than bright, it was dazzling.

I've Seen the Future and It Works

Over the course of the 80s things had been getting bigger. Waistlines, wallets, cars, hair, shopping centres... Everywhere we looked the world was expanding around us. When we had started the decade we were in a cosy yellow semi, snuggled into a cosy little estate. Without constant screens to stare at time moved slower, we noticed more of the environment around us and appreciated objects and detail, collecting things for ourselves to treasure as we travelled through the decade. We knew our towns and its streets by memory and not sat nav. We still shopped in local shops, where the storekeepers knew our names and no one rushed us on if we wanted to chat or spend five minutes choosing a ten-pence sweet mix, one careful decision at a time. We had only seen mall-style shopping centres on television and never thought for a moment we would ever see them here.

Our parents and grandparents were proud and excited to have left their working-class roots and hardships behind and landed in the sea of material heaven. We had reached heights that previous generations could have only dreamed about. Now, the dreams of our ancestors had become expectations for us and there would be no looking back. Growing up in the

80s meant that our futures could be fastened in a safety net as long as we didn't get too greedy and swept up with hedonism.

Being a girl in that decade meant that my education would not be expected to end after secondary school and marriage. I could be as successful as one of the boys if I wanted to be. I could get my name on a plaque at my school, I could improve the lives of women without being subjected to mockery, I could even earn enough money to buy myself every bit of Star Wars memorabilia available and have a shopping spree, even if it wasn't my birthday. Life was looking promising.

We were aware, unlike any generation before us, that the future was ours and anything was possible. 'The world is your oyster' was something we heard quite often from teachers and our parents, whether they were encouraging us towards university, or discussing the merits of seeing Madonna at Wembley arena.

I knew that my parents' work options had been limited by gender and something called the 'eleven-plus exam'. My dad had failed and so went to a secondary modern school which destined him for a manual occupation. My mom had passed and done well at grammar school but any dreams of further education had been crushed because of the need to contribute towards her keep. Besides, she would only get married and have children and what use was further education after that?

A generation before that, Nanny Pearl and Grandad Jimmy had both left school at fourteen for factory work because careers and businesses were for the sons of affluent families, unless you were prepared to face huge prejudices. A few years later conscription and wartime restrictions were to cut their freedoms short. Consequently they had always lived for the present and the concept of 'Where do you see yourself in five years' time?' which was what we were constantly being asked in school, was quite ridiculous. When I asked Grandad Jimmy the same question he gave me a strange look and said, 'How the bloody hell should I know?' whereas we were expected to give ambitious answers about 'career plans' and aspirations to travel.

By contrast to these earlier generations, our spare time was full of hedonism without a thought for the consequences, whether that be exploring for miles around us on our bikes all day as young kids, or as teenagers spending a weekend hunting down any opportunity to access alcohol and drink it without being caught in a time when such things were still quite easy to do. We would then lay out on the grass in whatever field or open space that beckoned and enjoy the feeling of freedom that came with no responsibilities (or sometimes the dizzy euphoria that a bottle of Diamond White or Thunderbird gave us). On Mondays we would be back in school, generally on our best behaviour, with eyebrow-raising stories and notes, carefully passed around the classrooms, about who had done what, said what and managed to get away with it. In a world before everyone had mobile phones and digital cameras it was very easy to get away with a lot of things. Many an 80s kid lied to their parents about having an innocent sleepover, when in reality they were half-dying of alcohol poisoning in a field somewhere, or about how they had been to the park when they had really cycled five miles to the woods and made a den and a real fire.

The 80s gave my mother, like many women who had been denied their potential early on, a second chance of a life outside the kitchen and selfless childcare duties. The Open University paved the way for careers, financial independence and all-

172

round better quality lives. The 80s enabled my primary school teacher, Miss McCoughney, to juggle marriage, motherhood and her career and to work her way up to be a head teacher. They even eventually enabled that ridiculous secondary school plaque to be removed and replaced with a long list of business women, professionals and philanthropists who had passed through its doors at some point during that decade.

The decade also gave my grandparents and many of their generation the opportunity to enjoy a retirement without poverty, previously unheard of for the working classes. They were living their own dream in their tasselled palace, surrounded by G-Plan and Royal Doulton limited editions. They had a chest freezer in their garage with enough meat and puddings inside to make up for all that rationing had denied them and every week they dressed up and treated themselves to a gammon and steak lunch at the Berni Inn, each time with such delight that it could have been their first outing.

As for me and Tony, and our contemporaries, we are now mostly responsible homeowners, hard workers, parents and law-abiding citizens. We talk of the 80s like they were a great film that we starred in. From our BMX tricks, to our nights out in the open, our petty crimes and a general absence of health and safety, the 80s were a decade of risk-taking, pleasure-seeking and dreams. It was the also the final decade before technology and social media started its mass takeover and we are grateful to have been part of it, although we are probably more grateful that, unlike our children's generation, there is no social media evidence to prove that we were there.

Printed in Great Britain
by Amazon

76580906R00102